ABOUT THE

Penny Haslam is an award-winning motivational speaker, coach and trainer who works with organisations and individuals to help them build their brand profile and get known for what they do.

As a former BBC business journalist, she regularly appeared on national television and radio, presenting the daily business news. Prior to presenting, she was a senior broadcast journalist, producing business and personal finance programmes on BBC Radio 4.

Penny left broadcasting in 2013, when she was invited by Weight Watchers to be one of its celebrity brand ambassadors for the year. She then started her own business in 2014, with a mission to help people power up their profile – and rid the world of dull speakers, boring panel discussions and uninspiring television and radio interviews.

In her talks and keynotes, Penny is insightful and funny (she's been dubbed 'a female Michael McIntyre, who speaks to business'). She holds a light up to the human condition of not wanting to look or feel like an idiot, giving her audiences practical and instantly usable take-aways, to raise their profile and boost their confidence.

pennyhaslam.co.uk
@pennyhaslam

MAKE YOURSELF
A LITTLE BIT FAMOUS

How to power up your profile and
get known for what you do

Penny Haslam

Make Yourself a Little Bit Famous:
How to Power Up Your Profile and Get Known for What You Do

ISBN 978-1-912300-27-3
eISBN 978-1-912300-28-0
Published in 2019 by SRA Books

Printed in the UK by TJ International Ltd, Padstow, Cornwall

CONTENTS

ACKNOWLEDGEMENTS

I have loved writing this book, I hope you can tell, but of course I'd not have got anywhere without love and support from my family.

My husband Steve has been the wind beneath my wings. Thank you for your endless cheerleading, chapter reviewing and poached eggs on toast (on a tray!!!). I honestly would not be the kick-ass woman I am today without you.

I am also very grateful to our girls for showing more than a modicum of interest. The youngest, whose keen interest in authors and their craft meant she was a great help in researching the quotes and book cover ideas and reminding me that J.K. Rowling was rejected many times before eventual success.

And the eldest was in charge of accountability, ensuring I stopped talking about it and actually got on with it. How could I not put finger to keyboard when I heard 'How's your book coming along, Mum?', practically every day? I'd have felt like a right loser had I not risen to the challenge.

Thank you, gang. Love you.

PREFACE

I have been a little bit famous. Why? How? Well, I used to be on television, bringing the country the latest news from the world of business and personal finance. Well, get me.

I could be found on a daily basis standing in front of a big screen, with a line graph of the FTSE100, saying things like 'the markets are up'. Or 'the markets are down'. Gripping stuff, I know.

I got up silly early for my shifts on the BBC's morning news programme, *Breakfast*, and its 24-hour rolling news channel, the rather creatively and aptly named News Channel. I piled on make-up, poured myself into block colour 'bodycon' dresses, bouffed my hair and smiled at the camera. I was just a jobbing freelance journalist, filling in when the staff presenters were on holiday, but I was at the very top of the tree of national network broadcasting.

Blink and you'd have missed me. Unless of course you actually like the business news and actually want to know about the highs and lows of the FTSE100, inflation figures and whether the British high street is going to hell in a handcart.

You'd have to have a good visual memory too, as it was quite a while ago that I was 'a little bit famous', for just a few years from 2011.

Anyway, before this short period of micro-stardom, I had been a behind-the-scenes business journalist for almost 12 years. At the height of my career I worked as a senior producer at BBC Radio 4, on programmes such as the weekly personal finance programme *Money Box* and the daily consumer show *You and Yours*. I also had a stint as a reporter on *Shop Talk*, a lightweight 'business for softies' programme (as we affectionately referred to it) that aired on Tuesday afternoons.

I was employed by the Radio Business Programmes Unit, at Broadcasting House and Television Centre, which came under the formidable umbrella of BBC News and Current Affairs.

And as you might expect, I loved it. I loved the variety, the opportunities and my colleagues (well, most of them). And, at the end of it all, I found myself to be a little bit famous.

But being on TV every day didn't float my boat as much as you'd think it would. Although I interviewed, on an almost daily basis, the great and good from the world of commerce during that time, I didn't have a clue about actually being in business.

The interviews were short and just scratched the surface, there wasn't the time to expand and I craved more. The challenges that the bulk of British businesses face weren't dealt with on TV or radio, as there wasn't the appetite for nuance.

The thing that I wanted most, the itch I couldn't scratch, even in the loftiest and most glamorous of jobs in TV news, was to be in business myself.

Fledgling entrepreneur

Long before I found broadcasting and journalism, I had had a stab at entrepreneurialism. Not that I had ever heard that word back then.

As a teenager, growing up in the UK in a suburb near Stockport, I paid the grand sum of 15p a week to place a postcard advert in our local newsagent's window. I offered babysitting, cleaning and ironing at £5 an hour for a variety of local customers.

I continued in this line of business when I went to university, successfully too, as I had more time between lectures to provide my services. I even employed a fellow student to help me when the piles of ironing became too much.

But by the time I was in full flow in my BBC career, that was just a distant memory. However, the entrepreneurial urge was always there and I desired the freedom of being my own boss.

To me, recognising a problem, offering a solution and then making money from it is very exciting – almost magical. The whole 'how you do that' fascinates me. Taking on staff, producing goods, offering services, creating a culture, distributing, selling online, doing deals, contracts, negotiating, testing the market, expanding, exporting…

You've got to agree, it is dizzying. And that's why I *thought* I loved business journalism. It was the closest I could get, at the time, to actually being in business.

From there to here

In 2013, I faced a delicious decision to make about my future, which resulted in me cutting ties with the BBC via a lucrative contract with Weight Watchers, to be one of its celebrity brand ambassadors. As yer do.

Their communications department rang me one day and said: 'We've seen you on TV and it's not that we think you are fat… but… Would you like to lose weight and star in an advert, made by Saatchi and Saatchi, alongside Patsy Kensit and Greg Wallace, that bald bloke off *MasterChef*?'

And I *was* overweight. I'm 5' 2' and had been carrying a lot of post-baby weight to the tune of size 18. Admittedly the baby was six years old by this time, so I may have been in denial.

Right away I said yes to the offer and after almost 20 years of dealing in serious business news, I was having fun. I got paid to lose weight (hello!) and, crucially, I slowly started to remember who I was and what I wanted out of life.

The year's promotional activity for Weight Watchers ended and I found myself at a junction: go back to broadcasting, somehow, or release my entrepreneurial flair on the world.

I chose the latter, and now, after a couple of false starts, I run my own business as a professional speaker. This means I am audacious enough to strut stages delivering hilarious and useful keynotes and talks, which have won me awards.

And I don't just talk on stages: people come to me for training and coaching to help them raise their profile and share their knowledge with more people. I show them how to ace a television or radio interview; how to be awesome on panels, either as a panellist or as the panel chair; and how to put a brilliant talk together and confidently deliver it.

I help employees, leaders, top teams and those doing their own thing with the strategy and skills they need to raise their profile. Hence the book.

Being in business

At first, my business acumen was all over the place. But over time I've gone from keen but green to confident and canny. And when I say 'at first', I mean for a good three years before it clicked, and I knew what the hell I was doing.

So, what's the point of telling you all of this, given this is a business book called *Make Yourself a Little Bit Famous* to help *you* raise your profile – and not my autobiography?

Well, the most important and useful learning during those early days, when I flew the BBC nest, was the lesson about 'getting out there'. Not just on an ad hoc 'oh, I think I'd better go to a networking thing' basis, but in a conscious and strategic way.

I had to find ways to make myself a little bit famous, now that I was responsible for finding paying customers. Being known as a barely famous ex-TV presenter simply didn't appeal to me. The words 'washed up' and 'has been' are fairly unavoidable in that narrow role.

I wanted to be more than just that. I wanted to find a way of having an impact and enabling others to do the same.

So, you might be part of a company or organisation that wants a better connection with its audiences – your customers, clients, candidates, investors, shareholders, stakeholders, partners and policy makers.

Engaging the services of marketing or PR agencies, or piling more pressure (often of the digital kind) onto in-house teams is expensive and results in a one-way conversation. Your brand is pushed at your audiences, when you try to sell and promote what you do. There are hungry and keen individuals within your organisation right now, champing at the bit to share their enthusiasm for what they do – so why not enable them to be your brand ambassadors?

Audiences these days want a more genuine interaction and engagement, if they're going to buy into what you do and what you stand for; they want you to speak *to* them, not *at* them.

Regardless of what you do, what you want to achieve or your experience thus far, you might have a hunch that playing on a bigger, or different, pitch might just serve your business or your career well. In fact, it might really suit you.

INTRODUCTION

Right then, who wants to be really famous!? No? In that case, do you want to be a best-kept secret? No, of course you don't!

So, welcome to the middle ground – and the book that helps you get out there, build your brand profile, and make yourself a *little* bit famous.

If you want to be known, liked and trusted, then this book is for you and most people realise this is important for business, leadership or career success.

But many of us only remember about raising our profile every now and again, in a sporadic, hit-and-miss sort of a way. We throw some mud at the wall, by going to a networking event once in a blue moon, and we hope that mud sticks. Or you might have spoken at one a couple of years back, and not been asked again. The impression you're left with is that it's all fairly pointless.

Time plays a big part in this too. You are undoubtedly time poor, with a thousand things to do before lunchtime. And with myriad ways to 'get out there' it can be overwhelming. You could fill every hour of every day using social media, video, blogging, emailing, speaking at events, taking part in panels, going to networking or appearing on the radio or television.

And the real truth of the matter is that most people are not sure of themselves in front of more than a few other people. They worry that they'll say the wrong thing, come across badly, not be liked, be hated, become a pariah in society and die alone. OK, just some of that is realistic, but that's quite often the deep-seated reason for holding yourself back.

So, you dodge it. You pass the buck to a colleague, tell

yourself you don't have time, and besides who wants to listen to what you've got to say anyway? But then you wish it was you up on the stage speaking, taking part in a panel discussion, or being asked for your opinion on TV or radio.

We know we need to participate in activities that will help draw attention to us. We know that we can't be a best-kept secret *and* attract customers, candidates, investors, partners, stakeholders and impress our connections and colleagues. But, and this is the rub, we are reluctant to draw attention to ourselves.

So, this book is for you if:

▶ You work for yourself, for someone else or are a leader – in any capacity.
▶ You realise that getting exposure will help you create opportunities, make connections and give you greater credibility.
▶ You or your organisation have a message to share and you want to have more influence and get heard.
▶ You want to develop a strategy to raise your profile that gets you nearer to where you want to be.

And this book is for you if you hold yourself back because you don't want to look like an idiot. My aim is to help you with the practical side of things and give you inspiration for getting on with it. It is all my best stuff – all the information and techniques and tips and practical knowledge that I share with my clients in my coaching and training sessions. So have it, take it all, and stop being a best-kept secret.

WHY
YOU SHOULD MAKE YOURSELF A LITTLE BIT FAMOUS

When you make yourself a little bit famous, you're going to get a little bit of attention. Forget being fully famous in a Kim Kardashian or *Britain's Got Talent* sort of a way, because that would be silly. What we're dealing with here is just getting known, a bit, and in a wholesome, respectable, enduring sort of a way.

The aim is to get attention from the people who matter to you, the ones you want to inform, influence and maybe even inspire. You'll want to get in front of them in order to help your career along, get budget or 'buy-in' for the stuff you're working on, and/or boost your business or organisation's brand.

For example, your list of who you should be seen by might include some of the following:

▶ Your customers or clients
▶ Your boss
▶ Your team
▶ The board
▶ Candidates
▶ Partners or stakeholders
▶ Influencers in your network
▶ Suppliers
▶ The wider industry
▶ Your investors
▶ Policy makers.

And of course, your *potential* customers, clients, colleagues, suppliers, and so on, who will also see you doing your thing and be impressed.

Before we jump into *how* you could make yourself a little

bit famous, it's worth spending a moment to think about why you should do it in the first place. Knowing this can spur you on and help you think more objectively about the activities you'll hear about in the practical chapters later on.

chapter 1

THE **WHY** IS IN THE **PIE**

Why should you bother with this make yourself a little bit famous malarkey? Why even think about 'getting out there' and getting known? It's a lot of effort, with high potential for looking and feeling like a complete idiot.

For me, the 'why' you should make yourself a little bit famous can be found in the model PIE (I'll explain this shortly). It comes in the form of a pie chart funnily enough and, indeed, we will be looking at the 'slices of the pie' through this next story about an appraisal I had when I was an employee at the BBC. I aim to exhaust all pie and slice related puns before the end of the chapter.

Now, as yet, I've not met anyone who says they enjoy appraisals. I mean, did you punch the air the morning of your last one? 'Hurrah, it's appraisal day! I get to set my objectives for the next 12 months!'

No, you did not. I was the exact same when I worked at the BBC as an employee (as opposed to when I worked there as a freelancer, joyfully appraisal free). They're the blight of our working lives, as far as I can see, and I hated 'appraisal season'.

For those fortunate enough to have never had the pleasure of an appraisal, let me explain. They are usually annual or six-monthly sit-downs with your line manager or boss, where you review the work you're doing, the job you've been employed to carry out.

You are assessed on whether or not you have met your objectives from the previous 12 months, set at last year's appraisal, and then you set some objectives for the 12 months ahead.

Sometimes the organisation's values or objectives come up, and you chat about whether or not you (a) understand them and (b) have met them. I know, scintillating stuff.

None of this ever struck me as a particularly useful way of assessing how well I was doing in my career. As a broadcast journalist I didn't sell or produce tangible things, so measuring the success of my work and efforts in my job was incredibly subjective.

I made a personal finance programme that was broadcast to the nation once a week on BBC Radio 4, at lunchtime on Saturdays. Fans among you will know that programme as *Money Box*.

I worked in a small, diligent team and was responsible for compiling a programme that incorporated the most up-to-date and accurate personal finance news. It had to be informative, educational and, when we could make it so, entertaining.

My team included a broadcast assistant, a researcher, a reporter and the presenter. It was my job to liaise with my editor and my counterparts on other Radio 4 programmes to make sure we weren't repeating subjects they planned to cover during the week.

I dealt with and interviewed government ministers, captains of industry and many of our listeners who wrote to or rang the programme with their stories. And I did all of this really well but, year to year, my salary (which is why we tend to turn up to appraisals, in the hope of a raise) stayed very much the same.

I felt stuck. I couldn't see how I could get more traction for my career (and my salary) or what I could do to improve my situation. As far as I could tell, when it came to being seen as somebody who deserved a pay rise, I was invisible.

So, as you can imagine, this particular appraisal was hardly setting the world alight. My line manager must have been a bit desperate to motivate me and so became the most animated

I'd ever seen him. He jumped up out of his chair, whipped out his flip chart and a big marker pen and drew a pie chart that looked something like this:

Now I'm guessing that my line manager, who had just come back from a leadership away day, had been told about PIE there. He said:

'Penny, you need to think differently about your career from now on. You need to think about the big picture, otherwise you're going nowhere...'

Charming.

He told me that I needed to think about the effort and energy I put into my career and that PIE would show me the way. So, what do P, I and the E stand for?

Well, this is how it was explained to me, by my line manager, back in 2002:

'P is for performance. Spend no more than 25 per cent of your efforts and energy on your performance.'

PERFORMANCE 25%

Twenty-five per cent!? A teeny-weeny quarter of my efforts and energy spent on my performance? Whaaaat?! I found this terribly disconcerting, as most people do when I tell them about this. It turned my world upside down, because wasn't that all there was to my role and my career?

I worked hard and had the right skills and abilities to perform my job, week in week out. And that was why I had been employed in the first place. I made radio programmes and I made them really well. So, performance, to my mind, was everything. Wasn't it?

Not so, according to my line manager, and he went on to explain: 'I is for image. Just 25 per cent of your efforts and energy should be spent on your image.'

IMAGE 25%

Woah, there! Image? Image! Why the hell does it matter what I look like? How offensive! I don't have an image to maintain, but nonetheless I scrub up quite nicely for work thank you very much. Besides, no one can see you on the radio.

That wasn't what he meant.

'It's about your image in your role, your career. How others see you, performing. Do others think you can do your job well? What's your reputation like?'

I was slightly stumped. Being completely honest, I didn't know.

'And, crucially,' he went on to say, 'what is your self-image like? Do you have good self-esteem?'

All very interesting, and intriguing. But what on earth could the remaining 50 per cent of your efforts and energy at work be spent on? What could be the E?

He finally revealed to me, in the appraisal that had been, until now, deathly dull:

'E is for exposure! Do you see, Penny? *Half* of your effort and energy should be spent getting exposure for your great performance and amazing image!'

EXPOSURE 50%

Exposure! What the… ?!

A whopping 50 per cent effort and energy was required, more than for anything else, to get exposure. He was telling me in no uncertain terms to get out there, and get known! I was now tasked with sharing my amazing performance at work and my great image.

I got it. It made sense. And when I share this story in my talks and keynote speeches, the audience gets it too! But had my boss given me instantly usable information? Not one bit. None of what he said could be put into practice. The reality was that this appraisal had taken place at a time when there simply weren't that many opportunities to 'get out there' and get exposure.

In fact, the only opportunity I had to get exposure was at the office Christmas party. I could expose myself as much as I liked.

But that was awkward. I could sidle up to an editor of one of the programmes we made or the line manager's manager. Or maybe even the big boss him or herself.

And I could say: 'Hi, I'm Penny. I produce *Money Box*. I do it well and other people think I do it well.'

Even if I had done that, I doubt it would have got me anywhere.

To me, it was networking without purpose, but with seemingly loads of pressure. It felt awkward and elevator pitchy. I didn't make stuff (measurable through productivity) and I didn't flog stuff (measurable through sales), so evidencing my great performance and image was hidebound in subjectivity.

It also feels like 'schmoozing', or sucking up to the boss, and at that time it was certainly quite un-female to 'brag' or 'boast' about your achievements.

The opportunities for getting exposure, or getting out there, were few and far between. There was no culture of belonging to an official in-house network, like many large firms have now. We didn't think about attending external networking events back then. And social media was non-existent. Imagine! No LinkedIn, no Twitter, no Instagram!

But it's a different story today as there are so many places to share what you do, and be useful, interesting, engaging.

I've since learned that my line manager had adapted PIE from the book *Empowering Yourself: The Organizational Game Revealed* by Harvey J. Coleman. He didn't even reference it, or suggest I read it! Frustratingly, he had shown me the theory, but had failed to give me any of the tools for getting the exposure I needed and deserved.

That of course gave me a great excuse for *not* making myself a little bit famous – but we are far from the time of my last BBC appraisal and you, my friend, don't have any excuses...

chapter 2

GET STUCK
INTO **PIE**

The 'why' is most definitely in the PIE, and in the next chapter we get into more detail about what you actually say when, er, exposing yourself. It's my model for preparing punchy and to-the-point communication, and it's called FACE.

You'll have noticed that I have exercised a huge degree of self-control by not bolting those two words together. That's not to say I haven't tried, but it turns out calling someone a 'pieface' isn't particularly flattering.

But before we work with my FACE, we need to get stuck into PIE. You see, intellectually, rationally, PIE is not difficult to understand. It makes sense, doesn't it? Get Exposure for your great Performance and Image, and you'll no longer be a best-kept secret. You'll then be well loved and rich beyond your wildest dreams.

But emotionally there's more to PIE than meets the eye, and it's easy to stray and stay in just one of the areas – hovering a bit too long in Performance for example, as I will show you in a moment.

So, sit back and enjoy another couple of stories, before you actually have to think about anything that causes anxiety dreams and makes your heart pump a little faster (like speaking in public, or going on live television).

Here's PIE, served up, one slice at a time…

P is for performance: stop colouring in!

We hide in the performance quarter. We lurk in this 25 per cent a bit too much. We make sure everything is all a bit Goldilocks (just right) before we launch whatever it is, on the world. Our i's have got to be dotted, beautifully. Our t's crossed at perfect right angles. And that stuff can hold us back.

I've been guilty of this myself and I have to watch myself on this all the time. Performance over-perfection usually shows up as something on your to-do list that never seems to get finished, launched and 'out there'.

Here are some examples of those things:

▶ a website you're building
▶ a book you're writing
▶ a report/dissertation/article/blog that needs submitting
▶ a conversation you want to have
▶ a group you want to set up
▶ a meeting that needs scheduling
▶ a speech you'd like to give
▶ a CV you want to upload
▶ an organisation you'd like to join
▶ or an email you need to send.

Yes, even an email you need to send.

Essentially, hiding in Performance, telling ourselves that we can't possibly take action because we're busy working on or thinking about 'that thing', is what stops us from moving on. We can feel stuck at a stage in our development, or business or career growth, because we're polishing and perfecting.

But we can iron this out through my embarrassing email story. It's embarrassing because it took me three months to write. Not full time, I'm not that slow, but I spent far too long on it.

The purpose of the email was to tell my contacts what I do and how I might help them. I wanted them to know that I wasn't just an ex-BBC presenter, but I now worked as a keynote speaker and event host, and was someone who could help them raise their profiles.

Oh, the irony.

And this email really needed to get sent, because I really needed to drum up some business, in order to pay the mortgage and feed the family. But three months of dragging it around with me, working on it, thinking about it, worrying that it wasn't good enough, was what you might call puh-*thet*-ick!

So, what was causing the delay? Well, on the surface, I was fannying around getting to grips with which database to use, which email service to sign up to, and then how to work that database and email service. Then I was dilly-dallying with my logo and headshot. Then, where should they be placed (left, right or centre) on the template of my email? Then, I spent time fiddling with how to use the email newsletter software that wasn't at all intuitive.

And of course, I laboured over the words to write, how to convey a light touch but with a strong call to action. I wanted to come across as casually positioned with one elbow on the fireplace, airily offering guidance to a rapt audience of readers. I didn't want to come across as show-offy, or self-centred. In short, I was three months down with nothing to show for it.

So, I rang my friend Gail who knows about these things. I met Gail about ten years ago, when I saw her speak at a conference. She runs her own successful business selling ladders and has a very pragmatic head on her shoulders. No lofty ideas from Gail. (I'm here all week.)

I told Gail that my idea for spreading the word about what I do and how I can help people had come to a standstill, and that it probably wasn't meant to be, and that I'd pay my mortgage through other means – because this really wasn't working.

She listened to my sad, pathetic story and said:

'Penny Haslam, you are colouring in.'

I looked down at my shoes and, in the pregnant pause that followed, I sighed. She went on:

'You are colouring in, all the way up to the edges, making sure everything is just right and just so. You've got out all your little colouring pens and their lids, and they're lined up in rainbow order, while you neatly make sure you're not going over the lines.

'But all of this means you're avoiding the one thing that will really help you. So, may I suggest you stop colouring in – and sketch your future?!'

Stop colouring in, and sketch your future. *My* future. Gulp.

I hadn't anticipated that, although I should have, because Gail is a straight-talking businesswoman who can spot a colourer-inner at a hundred paces.

And I realised that, rather annoyingly, she was right. I had been lurking in that first 25 per cent of PIE. I had spent too long sitting in my own P, as it were. Perfecting the performance of it all, procrastinating because ultimately, deep down, I was afraid. I was afraid I would get 'found out' and look like an idiot. I admitted it, and I said to her:

'I am afraid I will fail, Gail.'

But after Gail's intervention, I pressed send on my embarrassing email that afternoon and had three immediate responses, all of which were positive. In one reply, I was asked for a quote to host a conference.

I had been colouring in, when I should have been sketching my future. Colouring in, with a big fat useless pencil case full of pens and pencils, stuffed with those transparent plastic protractors and right-angle things that no one needs, and a whole heap of equally pointless excuses about 'getting it just right'. I had indeed been colouring in.

My lesson is this: do not do this.

I is for image: call yourself an expert!

My line manager had asked me in that appraisal: what's your image? I had no idea. Had he been more helpful, he might have gone on to suggest I think about adopting an area of expertise and delving into that, in order to create a stronger image.

When I deliver my Make Yourself a Little Bit Famous keynotes and talks, I ask audience members to put up their hands if they consider themselves to be an expert. Barely anyone puts their hand up, unless they are already labelled as such – like a lawyer, doctor or accountant – and can lay claim to being 'expert' because their certificate says so.

So few people consider themselves as such, even when they know absolutely tons about their stuff. I've met neuroscientists, HR directors, authors of business books, CEOs of national organisations, who do not declare themselves 'expert' and in fact say that they don't know as much as their peers.

But positioning your image as 'expert in something' can bear fruit. I wish I'd focused on it sooner and got some help and ideas about it, as my career and my confidence would have benefited enormously. Why? Well, it helps other people understand what it is you do, what you're passionate about, and why you're the person, or organisation, who can help. It gives you a strong selling point in the marketing of your skills and experience, or what you offer as a business.

Being associated with a subject that you know lots about hands you far more to go at than simply being associated with a personality trait or skillset.

For example, is your image primarily based around a one-dimensional term such as she/he is 'hard working', 'thorough', 'good at detail', 'funny', 'assertive' and so on? It's a bit thin if that's the case and won't serve you very well, over a longer period of time.

Since being in business myself, and growing up a bit, I see now that I'd not paid any attention to this area of my career – to my image. When I worked at the BBC on Radio 4, I was in personal finance journalism but didn't want the image of 'personal finance person' to stick and so distanced myself from it. And besides, the people around me knew so much more than me. *They* were the real subject specialists – so who was I to identify as such? I know now that this is a common comparison which inhibits people from seeing the expertise that they do have, and is useful to others.

But it's as simple as how the Oxford English Dictionary defines it: an expert is 'a person who is very knowledgeable about or skilful in a particular area'.

If you look upon 'experts' in that way – as people who know some stuff, are experienced and passionate – you'll see that ordinary people with careers or businesses can fashion themselves as experts.

Expertise doesn't have to stop with the job in hand, the work you do or your core business. It can expand to be more useful, to more people. Expertise can be based on your experience, and draw on a wide range of things.

More than just an IT guy

David Miller is the owner of Miller Waite, an IT firm in Cumbria in the north of England that employs around 20 people; the firm's clients operate in different sectors and range in size.

He is currently advertising for apprentices, and focusing on gender diversity as they currently employ mostly men – and David has a plan to double the size of his company over the next two years.

David's expertise, on the surface, could simply be about information and technology, how companies use data, how they structure it and keep it super cyber-safe.

And yes, David could spend all day talking about that and sometimes does. His expertise on that level is quite obvious and indeed it is useful, directly to customers and employees.

But David is also knowledgeable, experienced and passionate in:

► Business growth – whether his clients are expanding or buying IT that will support future growth.
► Latest legislation or data regulation and how it affects different sectors and organisations.
► New technology and whether it's to be trusted or not.
► Cyber-attacks on big firms that make the news headlines.
► Apprenticeships and government schemes to support employment and skills.
► Engaging employees, and retaining them.
► Diversity and inclusion in the workplace.
► Skills shortages in STEM (science, technology, engineering and maths).

Can you come up with a list like this, based on your job, the type of work you do, or area of business you come across? You can draw on what you see and hear along the way too.

If you're unsure of your expertise you could start by asking yourself some of the following questions:

▶ What elements of the work you do interest you the most and light you up when you talk about them?

▶ What do you know a lot about, not necessarily more than a colleague or competitor, but more than the average person?

▶ What do people come to you for and how do you help them, or enhance their lives?

Don't worry if you can't answer those questions right now – put them on your back-brain burner, on simmer, so the answers can be cooking while you do other things.

Had someone asked me those questions, I might have said that I was someone who was passionate about clear and effective communication, be it specifically making a weekly radio programme, or communicating clearly with my team for a smooth-running show. That's what interested me most, not the personal finance news or the journalism for its own sake. If I'd had to think about it more deeply, I could well have developed and showcased my transferrable skills more effectively and perhaps moved on more quickly in my career.

It may seem obvious but I'll state it anyway: make sure you align your expertise with what you want to achieve. Put the subject area that supports your objectives front and centre. If you want to advance your career, highlight an area of expertise that will help your organisation the most. If you want more customers, highlight your expertise which shows you understand their problems.

The wonderful by-product of nailing your expert colours to the mast is that you get to know more about your subject area. In turn, the more expert you become. You're naturally drawn to information about your topic and people begin to send you information, include you in conversations associated with it. Expertise gathers momentum, so if I is for Image, what do you want yours to be?

E is for Exposure: run for mayor!

I met a bloke a couple of years ago who'd invented a chewing gum. Yes, a chewing gum. He seemed nice enough and was attending a big four-day conference shindig event for successful entrepreneurs. He'd travelled from Canada to Monaco to essentially network with other entrepreneurs and learn what he could from them.

Was I there in the hot sun of Monaco, staying at the Fairmont Monte Carlo hotel, overlooking the hairpin bends of the Grand Prix because I myself was a successful entrepreneur? *Non!* I was there because one of the world's biggest accountancy firms had hired me as their business interviewer for the corporate videos they made about the event. My role was to interview a bunch of successful entrepreneurs about their successes, and failures, and to cut a long story short, one of my interviewees was that bloke from Canada, who'd invented a chewing gum.

Jay Klein had started out in 2010, working on a recipe for a chewing gum that was to be sugar free and aspartame free (aspartame is an artificial sweetener reported to be associated with cancer and heart disease). He called it PUR Gum.

I'm ashamed to admit that I was actually quite patronising towards him. Not out loud, but in my mind. My BBC business journalist's slightly pompous inner voice was saying, 'Aw, that's nice, inventing a little chewing gum. Bless his cotton socks.'

My mild disdain came from knowing the backdrop against which he was attempting to gain market share. How would Jay Klein – with his little chewing gum – stand a chance against the global mega brands? Did he not know that a whopping 75 per cent share of the global gum market is dominated by just three names – Wrigley in the US, Cadbury in the UK and Lotte in South Korea and Japan? Was he unaware the world's chewing gum industry is estimated to be worth approximately $19 billion?

Plus, the big players have it totally nailed with their research and product development, their marketing and distribution networks. How would this plucky Canadian entrepreneur, with PUR Gum, ever break into anything – let alone make any money from it?

So, I asked him, but held back on the condescending tone.

'Can you tell me about your plans or activity that helps you spread the word about your product?'

And straight off the bat he said:

'Penny, I am running for mayor! It's as simple as that. I'm taking my product and I'm going around the world, shaking hands, kissing babies and putting my chewing gum into the hands of the people who might sell it and those who might buy it!'

He continued: 'And my campaign issues are a lower-sugar diet and the dangers associated with aspartame, the artificial sweetener.'

Because, he went on to tell me, that's what people are interested in. They don't care about his chewing gum, really.

And he was spot on. Every January, in the press, we're told we've eaten too much sugar over Christmas (we have!). In the springtime, we're told to cut back on sugar to get beach-body ready (I'm always beach ready – towel, picnic, flask of tea). Research and reports tell us we're all going to be diabetic by the time we finish the newspaper article we're reading. And obesity hits the headlines almost every day, with calls to reduce the amount of sugar the food industry pours into processed foods.

It's the same with his other topic, aspartame. When anything related to it is mentioned – new findings or research – Jay jumps on it. He shares it, comments on it, writes about it, and can reference it in a talk or when he's on a panel.

The TV and radio people now know he's a good talker on those subjects, so ask him to share his expertise (simply, his knowledge, experience and passion) on their programmes, whenever they are covering those topics.

And just like a proper mayoral candidate, dealing in the concerns of their voters, Klein got lift-off for his gum by landing on what his customers cared about – not by banging the drum about his gum.

When I met him, the product was already being sold in over 50,000 locations in approximately 50 countries, and the PUR Company Inc was valued at $10 million.

I loved meeting him because he is the epitome of the PIE approach. This Canadian entrepreneur had sorted out the performance element with his product and he'd carved out an image for himself as an expert. He was getting exposure for both and it was paying off.

And Klein's 'running for mayor' strategy has resulted in more exposure than any PR or marketing plan could ever give him. He comments on the 'stuff' in the world that is of interest to many people; he doesn't try to be the story. He gets exposure for that and easily 'gets out there' with his topics, because it's not all about him. He is able to showcase his expertise, without feeling like a show-off.

And guess what: the gum sells itself.

Five top tips for making life as sweet as PIE

- ► Your performance is good enough. Don't seek performance perfection or you'll end up lurking in this slice of PIE too much.
- ► Fashion your image as an expert. What do you know about and have experience in – and is this your passion?
- ► Consider your campaign issues – what is your subject area specialism that's of use or interest to people?
- ► Think about where your campaign trail might be – who do you need to get in front of somehow?
- ► Write down what you could do to get more exposure over the next 12 months.

If you remember nothing else, remember this

Stop colouring in, and sketch your future.

chapter 3

INTRODUCING…
MY **FACE**

There's a great power in words, if you don't hitch too many of them together.

Josh Billings

Many people confess to me that they would love to get out there more, but hold themselves back because they 'don't know what to say'. Or, they tell me they're guilty of 'going on a bit', and don't know when to shut up.

Knowing 'what to say' can be remedied to a certain extent by dealing in your subject area – your expertise. But package that up into concise, compelling and confident communication, and you'll make yourself a little bit famous with no problem at all.

So, to the rescue: my FACE! Or rather, the acronym I came up with, for everything you need for a really cool bit of communication. You're welcome!

I teach FACE on my training courses and share it with my coaching clients. As such, people have used my FACE in all manner of situations. It's perfect for the audience Q&A section following a talk, or if you're taking part in a panel discussion, or when you're being interviewed on television or radio.

In meetings, it is very handy. Take my FACE with you to sound completely on top of your game. I've heard of it being used successfully in board meetings and at job interviews.

And it's not limited to use solely as a preparation tool for verbal communication; you can apply it to the written word too – an email, a blog or post on social media, for example. It is simply a way of packaging up what you want to get across, so you sound good and don't bore anyone.

FACE foundations

I came up with this model after years of interviewing people on TV and radio, and identifying what makes really good communication. As well as asking good questions, a journalist's job is to listen really well to the answers. And I listened during live interviews, and in my headphones when I edited the interviews that had been recorded.

The better of the interviewees, the ones we invited back, stood out as memorable and likeable. Why? Quite simply, they were concise, confident and compelling. But they had something else in common: their answers always included facts, additional information, comments and examples.

- ▶ **F**acts
- ▶ **A**dditional information
- ▶ **C**omments
- ▶ **E**xamples

Ta-dah!

And FACE was born. For a number of years, I only taught it as part of my media training, but found I was sharing it more and more with people who wanted to sharpen up their communication.

Short and to the point

On-air interviewees have two or three minutes on live TV news, or four to five minutes on a radio programme, to make an impact. In business, the parallel is a comment in a meeting, a corridor conversation, a pitch to a client, a phone call, or chatting at a networking event.

Making your point efficiently is vital in today's fast-paced world. If you think about it for a moment, most of our day-to-day communication has to be succinct. Very few people have time to read a dissertation when a paragraph will do.

In the written form, there's no hanging around. It's 280 characters for a tweet, a couple-of-sentences post on LinkedIn, or a 600-word blog.

With FACE, you can showcase your expertise and are in with a chance of 'cutting through the noise', as they say. And when you're under pressure or nervous, FACE brings out the good stuff and pops it into the front of your mind – so you're less likely to forget what you want to say. And that is so annoying, isn't it, when you walk away from a meeting, having forgotten to say that thing you wanted to say?

Later in the book, chapter 5 shows how to take part in panel discussions. On a panel, you're also limited by time, so it's important to get on with making your point, but making it with impact – so you're memorable and interesting to the audience.

One client, having learned to use FACE to prepare her thoughts, told me she was astonished at how much unstructured, undirected chit-chat there was in panel discussions.

If you haven't taken time to prepare your thoughts, there's a tendency to talk too much, while your brain catches up. You're in danger of telling what I call a 'Titanic-dote'.

A Titanic-dote is where you think the story you're about to tell is going to be brilliant. You set off on your journey, telling your tale, only to find it's too long, sinks and goes nowhere. And you know yourself when you're halfway through doing it.

Without focus, you miss the opportunity for landing your

message. Your sentences are flabby, your thoughts are woolly, and so you end up wasting your own airtime.

Given that most of our daily communication is brief and to the point, we should prepare and communicate as though we are actual 'on-air experts'.

How my FACE can work for you

I favour the back of an envelope, or scrap of paper, approach for jotting down ideas that fit the facts, additional information, comments and examples boxes.

FACT	ADD DETAIL
COMMENT What I'd say about that is…	EXAMPLE For example…

Facts

Facts are easy to come by and can quickly help establish your credibility as someone who is knowledgeable.

However, don't spend too long on coming up with a bunch of numbers that no one really wants to hear about. Think big, bold headline facts that are related to what you're saying. Facts don't need to be from surveys or research done by someone else – they could be from your own experience too. For example, '…around half of our trade customers are asking for longer payment periods, or to delay their invoices.'

In practice, you might not need any facts. I find that people are trading far more in stories and examples. For example, the financial services sector in the past might have bandied impressive growth figures about and been quite domineering about them. These days, they deal more in clients' stories and the positive impact their service and advice might have had on someone.

Nonetheless, it is a good idea to have some up your sleeve. You don't need to cite where they came from when you express them, but you might get asked about it later down the line. And please, whatever you do, don't make up stuff to say.

Additional information

This just means add a bit of detail about the fact you've mentioned – flesh it out a bit. You can say a bit more about the issue in hand from a factual point of view.

Comments

You are the expert, so you should have some things to say about the world from your perspective. This is a reminder that you should express them as part of your package of great communication.

Reveal your passion and energy for the subject matter in hand. What you think and feel about it. Are you pleased or horrified? Do you welcome what we're talking about or are you worried? Should we feel excited about the topic or change of circumstances, or threatened? What's going to happen if we do/don't take action?

When you share your opinions, you help people understand

what you stand for, who you are and why you're the person to listen to (and do business with). Keeping both buttocks clenched either side of the fence is not a good look.

Having said that, reflecting a range of opinion in this section is OK too. I was once invited on to an evening television news show, to talk about the forthcoming nuptials of Prince Charles and Camilla. Now I am indifferent to all aspects of the royal family, especially indifferent, if you can be such a thing, to the romantic shenanigans of the upper echelons of society.

But I knew I needed something more than just that to say on the live TV show, and fast! So, I phoned a friend. Well two actually. One who *loves* the royal family and thought it was wonderful news, and another who *hates* the royal family and detests any pomp and ceremony.

I reflected their views in my comments, and said something along the lines of '... it's like Marmite. Some people are all for it and they'll be glued to the telly on royal wedding day, and some people are really against it saying it's a waste of taxpayers' time and money. Personally, I don't care what they do with their love life, it's up to them...' and then went on a bit about dress fittings, and whether he'd wear a kilt.

Examples

If you want to hook people in to what you're saying, it's imperative you drum up examples to help make your point. I could call this element 'stories', and that's a popular theme in business thinking right now. But to me that indicates a beginning, a middle and an end. Once upon a time...

Useful in some circumstances I'm sure, but when you're short on time, you've got to cut to the chase. And besides, just a sprinkling, a flash, of a real-world example is enough to stimulate your listener's imagination with relatable, likeable content.

Couple your comments with some interesting, well-crafted examples from your own working world. You can illustrate the type of people/clients you work with, how you help them or the wider community. Your examples can also demonstrate how you succeeded or why you failed. Make sure they are relevant to what you're saying of course!

A word of warning: the example element of FACE is the hardest bit. I've not worked with anyone who can nail it straight away. Matching up a visual story example from your world that you can easily tell and that underpins what you're saying is not easy. Keep running through your Rolodex of visual ideas and experiences.

Also, your example doesn't need to be elaborate, but without any reference to the real world you become less relatable, less memorable – the cornerstones of making yourself a little bit famous.

How to use my FACE

Clearly, you're not going to put just anything down, so think of a scenario where you want to make a point – either at home or work. It might be an issue that regularly comes up or about an aspect of a project you're working on. Plot out some ideas onto the grid.

Make sure you have something in each of the quadrants, and double-check they are what you think they are. Facts easily get mixed up with opinion, in my opinion.

Let's say I need to prepare for an interview on television.

The art world's Turner Prize has just been won by a Scottish artist who used her smartphone to create video. It's something I encourage people to do, in order to raise their profile (make video, not win the Turner Prize necessarily), so have been asked to talk about it.

In the hours before the interview, I'd whip out a piece of paper, make a quadrant for FACE and fill in the boxes with some thoughts.

FACT	ADD DETAIL
Radio 4, reporter, dispatched to interview the inventor of SMS text messaging.	Nokia mobiles, 2001.
COMMENT	EXAMPLE
Wasn't excited. Couldn't see what all the fuss is about.	Small office, central London, books piled high, showed me video on a phone, Japanese students, ski slope, hello mum.

So that's my preparation, using FACE. It gets me thinking through what I might say, but doesn't have to come out of my mouth in that order.

How might it sound out loud then? Here's the Q&A:

Presenter: Do you have to know a lot about technology in order to use video on your phone?
Penny: Not at all! In fact, when I worked as a

radio reporter, I was once dispatched to interview the inventor of SMS text messaging. [Fact]

It was 2001 – we'd really only just started using mobiles. We were all on our Nokias, weren't we, playing Snake – no cameras on them, and well before smartphones were on the market. [Additional information]

But I wasn't at all bothered about going to interview him – I didn't get it, and still don't really. I've never been a fan of technology for technology's sake and I couldn't see what all the fuss was about. [Comment]

Anyway, the inventor's office was in central London, in a high-rise block, in a poky little office, a bit sweaty, packed with bookshelves and computers, journals piled high, and a few researchers staring at screens. [Example]

He showed me the 'latest thing' on his mobile phone. A screen, with a video playing on it! And the video that was playing was of a bunch of Japanese students, in ski gear, on top of a bright snowy mountain. And they were using video on their phones – holding them up in the sunshine, waving and saying 'hello mum'. [Example]

But just to show how much of a late adopter I am,

and why you don't need to be a tech smarty-pants to use smartphone video and win the Turner prize – I thought to myself, when I saw those students on his screen: 'What? Video on your phone? Pah, that will never take off!' [Comment]

So, what sprang to mind, when you were reading that? The sunny mountain, the inventor's office, perhaps? What did you relate to? My Luddite tendencies perhaps, or the humour. It's unlikely that you really remember the fact that I was a reporter or that I worked for Radio 4.

Plus, having prepared with FACE, I knew exactly what I should include – it was front of mind so no Titanic-dotes for me. Read that out loud and it will take around one minute and twenty seconds. FACE has helped me be ultra-lean on the time it takes to make the point that even idiots like me, with no technological interest, can use a camera on their phone to make a short video.

Make an impact with FACE

The top team at the Joseph Rowntree Foundation (JRF) in York appear a lot on TV and radio and take part in panel discussions. JRF researches poverty in the UK and ways to solve it. There's no time at all in which to make an impact, and talking about the numbers of people living in poverty isn't engaging.

I worked with JRF, helping them fashion real-world, human examples to paint pictures with words. Sparking interest and empathy helps them land their important message more effectively.

Before they might have said: '... there are 14.1 million

people living in poverty in the UK. Of these, 8.2 million are working age adults, 4.1 million are children and 1.9 million are pensioners...'

By spending time on some real-life examples, they might say: '... imagine going to the supermarket, picking up your basket and then having to decide whether you buy toothpaste because you've run out, or get food for the kids' tea that night...'

You can hear the difference, can't you? One turns you off, the other draws you in.

And it's more memorable. According to Dan Heath, co-author of *Made to Stick: Why Some Ideas Take Hold and Others Come Unstuck*, after hearing someone talk, 63 per cent of people can remember a story, while 5 per cent of people can remember a statistic.

Five top tips for using my FACE

▶ Gather examples you can use from everyday life and make a note of them.

▶ Rehearse your story examples out loud so they are pithy and make an impact. Try them out on unsuspecting friends and colleagues to see if they make sense.

▶ Be as down to earth and personal as you are comfortable with, because real, authentic people are far more likeable and relatable.

▶ Start articulating your opinions, or ask others for theirs.

▶ FACE doesn't have to be the order in which you say your stuff – it's a preparation tool.

If you remember nothing else, remember this

Always work on E for example first, as it's the hardest element of the FACE model.

HOW
YOU COULD
MAKE YOURSELF
A LITTLE BIT
FAMOUS

So, that was the 'why you should' section of the book. Now for the juicy bit, the 'how you could' make yourself a little bit famous.

The following chapters are your 'how-to' handbooks that will arm you with the skills you need when you've said yes to a profile-raising opportunity. You might be speaking in front of people, taking part in a panel discussion or being interviewed on television or radio.

They also give you suggestions for getting out there more and are designed to help you no matter what level you're at. You might have been on TV or taken part in a panel discussion, but didn't feel you made the most of the opportunity and want some extra knowledge to support you. Or you might have something coming up that you haven't got a clue how to approach – these chapters are on hand for whenever you need them.

I'm a very practical person and I draw on my experience as an award-winning professional speaker, as a panel chair and as a broadcaster.

I know what the very best looks and sounds like, and these handbooks reflect how I help my clients when I'm coaching or training them. Share the tips and techniques with colleagues and friends, and dip into the chapters to make yourself a little bit famous.

chapter 4

MAKE YOURSELF A LITTLE BIT FAMOUS... BY SPEAKING

I learned from my mother that if you have a chance to speak, you should speak.

Ursula Burns, CEO, Xerox

Speaking in front of people can be terrifying, but if you want to make yourself a little bit famous, this is a major weapon in your armoury.

You might be a complete novice and want to get started, or you may have some experience of speaking, but wish to improve and do more. Or, you want to go from 'good to great', to which I say hurrah, bring it on! I hope this chapter will serve you well, regardless of your level.

It is possible that your knee-jerk reaction to getting up in front of a room of people is that you would rather die. Maybe a colleague, or one of your team, expresses that whenever they're asked to do a presentation.

In a poll of 2,000 people, conducted on behalf of Ripley's Believe It or Not! museum in London, a fear of public speaking was found to be a more pressing concern than death. Top of the fear charts was the fear of losing a family member, number two was public speaking, and at third place was your own death.

But I reckon they asked the wrong people – not people who are keen to make themselves a little bit famous, in order to do more business, boost their careers, or be more visible as leaders.

Of course you're going to have some concerns about speaking in public! After childbirth, it's one of the least natural things you can do in life. This is what many of my clients say when we first get to work on their talks:

▶ 'I'm not expert enough.'

▶ 'My voice/accent is off-putting.'

▶ 'I don't know what to say.'

▶ 'I don't know where to start.'

▶ 'I won't make any sense.'

▶ 'I'll speak too fast/too slow.'

▶ 'I get so nervous I think I'll pass out.'

And, on a very practical note, 'I'll trip on the way to the stage.'

What they're telling me, of course, is that they are human. They are simply experiencing the very human fears of being rejected, and being unloved. Funnily enough, those fears come up a lot in all the 'fame-inducing' activity I cover in this book.

But if you're prepared to push past your basic human frailty, overlook the fears and do it anyway, then you can look forward to an exciting journey of developing your skills and abilities as a communicator.

Now, you might think that as a former broadcaster, transitioning to being a paid professional speaker would be a walk in the park for me, but it really wasn't. I didn't know where to start or what to say. I had spent my career writing about news stories, the shorter the better. I had then read scripts, either on paper in the radio studio, or on autocue while looking into the TV camera.

Going from looking at the words and saying them to looking at people and speaking totally did my head in. Plus, not having a news story to talk about meant I had to find my own stories.

What I'm saying is that I know speaking in public can be

a challenge, and it takes time and patience to be able to do it really well. But take speaking seriously and you will reap the rewards.

Why I started speaking in public

When I first left the BBC, in 2013, I started attending networking events. I had set up a business called Penny Haslam's Expert Women. The logo was in grey and yellow, and spelled out PHEW. (I loved that logo, although as it turned out, it was the best thing about the business.)

PHEW aimed to answer the broadcasters' new-found demand for getting more women experts on air and to help businesswomen take advantage of media opportunities to raise their profile.

I was under the impression that networking would help me 'take my business to the next level'. I'd been told it was a way to meet people – an opportunity to tell strangers how I could help them. Then we'd all skip off into the business sunset together.

Around this time, my husband had just taken voluntary redundancy from his reporter job at BBC Radio 5 Live. As I too had left a relatively regular stream of income as a broadcaster, this was not the wisest of financial planning decisions. It's fair to say we were a little stressed, but were doing our best to style it out.

So, there we were, huddling out of the rain at the entrance to this networking event in Manchester, clutching our freshly printed business cards that we planned to press into the paws of our soon-to-be amazing business connections.

My problem was that despite being all full of chat and smiles on TV, confident and happy to interview absolutely anyone, I just wasn't feeling it. I was nervous and worried that I wouldn't fit in. And having had a long career as an asker of questions, I felt out of control and shy. I didn't know what to say about myself and, bottom line, I was afraid of looking stupid.

I told my husband about my deep fears, insecurities and concerns and he did what any supportive spouse would do. He gently placed his hand in the small of my back and shoved me over the threshold, hissing 'Get in there, and bloody talk to people.'

I grabbed the first person I saw, gabbled on at her for 20 minutes and then remembered it was a networking event. So I asked her 'What do you do?' To which she replied, 'Oh, I'm not meant to be here, I was just getting a drink of water, I'm the photographer's assistant.'

Shake hands with everybody in the room

Not long after that, I was invited to speak at a networking event. Gosh. I'd not heard of that happening, or seen it at the events I'd attended. I cobbled something together about the importance of women being seen on TV and heard on radio as experts, and that the people in the room should think about doing it for themselves.

Admittedly it wasn't a comfortable experience. I got my mucking words fuddled, lost track of what I was talking about, smiled to cover it up and somehow made it through. I could have made so much more of the opportunity for sure. But afterwards, people came up to me to ask for my business card, to arrange a coffee meeting, to find out more.

And that was a lightbulb moment for me. I'm running a business, this is how I can get customers! If I was seen at the front, speaking, it would be like shaking hands with the whole room in one go. I should do this more, I thought, it would save me from my nightmare of networking.

Why you should speak

Like Guinness, speaking is good for you, as my lightbulb moment has indicated. You can inform your audience, influence them and hopefully inspire them. It's a quick way for people, in one sitting, to get to know you, like and trust you. It can work really well for your brand – whatever you choose that to be, personal brand or organisational brand. But it benefits different people depending on their circumstances:

Self-employed or business owners

If you run your own business, speaking should be in your marketing mix. Why just *attend* a networking or association event, when you can stand out in the crowd at the front of the room? People see you and want to work with you – or at least to find out more about how you can help them.

If you have content that's useful to the audience (rather than it just being about you and your business – be useful, not salesy), and a strong, clear message, you are more likely to be remembered favourably.

Set yourself a goal or target to speak at a certain number of events through the year.

Leaders

Being visible is paramount for modern leadership. You should be aiming to inform, influence and inspire the people around you. You might have practical information to convey to your staff, or thoughts that you hope will have an impact on policy makers, for example.

In-house, the people who look up to you need to know your vision and what their part in it might be. Share that, regularly and consistently, and your teams will know where you're all headed – and will be more engaged as a result. Don't hide away in your office. Your people simply won't know, like or trust you. And then they leave, and it's all your fault.

Presenting well in the boardroom can get you buy-in for your ideas, influence board members and trustees, and impress investors and clients.

And looking further afield, attending external events as a speaker gives you visibility for your brand's profile and thought leadership. When I work as an event moderator, I spend all day introducing speakers and watching them on stage. Many of them are so-called 'industry speakers' who are there to represent their business.

Employees

If you're an employee and have ambition for your career then your personal brand will benefit from speaking. You can offer to present information, show that you are willing and then have a really good go at it.

And one of the best ways to get visibility for your personal brand profile is to speak up at meetings. All it takes is to ask a question, input with some intel or underpin a point with a short anecdote – look again at my FACE in chapter 3 to prepare your thoughts before a meeting.

In her research, the author of *Speak with Impact: How to Command the Room and Influence Others*, Allison Shapira, found that speaking up at work is a requirement for emerging leaders. She interviewed group heads of large financial services companies and heard the same unequivocal comment again and again:

'If you are in the room for a meeting, we expect you to speak up.'

The wins are spectacular no matter what level of the organisation you're at: your kudos and credibility as an expert in your field. The very fact that you had the chutzpah to get up and speak is very impressive. If you do it well, gosh, imagine... you'd be a little bit famous, wouldn't you?

There's no dodging this stuff if you want to 'get on' at work – so embrace it, make it 'your thing'. Study it like it's an A level.

So, no matter who you are, or what you do, focusing on developing your speaking skills and strategy will pay off. Through practice, and dedication, get yourself to a point where you know what you're doing.

The unattainable and the downright terrible

When we think about speaking in public, most people jump to the image of being at the centre of a high stage. Bright lights are shining in their face, and of course it's in front of hundreds of people. You're trying to think of something to say... which is possibly the worst image you can conjure, as it prevents you from approaching speaking in a calm and sensible way.

But we also think of the unreachable image of the Steve Jobs-type business speaker, who's as cool as a cucumber. Or, an in-your-face motivational speaker, with a headset microphone positioned along their overly chiselled jawline.

We are in awe of people who seem to speak effortlessly in

front of rapt audiences. Maybe you have a boss who can talk eloquently, without cue cards, retaining important information while showing their human side at the same time. Or there's the sector colleague, or competitor, who's charismatic, intelligent and fluent in front of groups of people. How annoying.

Of course, it's a reasonable image to conjure up, because that's what we see in films, on television and on the Internet. You can watch a billion hours of TED talks, on any subject you like, with speaker after speaker looking like they know what they're doing. Again, highly irritating.

At the opposite end of the scale, there's the downright terrible, isn't there? We've all seen them – the person who stumbles and fluffs their way through a painful talk. Their neck flushes red from nerves, they are a bit sweaty. They talk too fast, or too slow. It's boring stuff they're saying too. And the whole audience cringes, as they watch the speaker's discomfort and slow death at the front of the room.

Then there's the middle ground: an 'OK' speaker, who's clearly prepared their talk – but has maybe gone into overdrive with the detail. They probably have a seemingly endless number of slides with numbers, graphs and bullet points that they insist on reading out. It's all a bit of a drag, but you can't quite put your finger on why. It was OK.

Now, I know that much of what we imagine about speaking, and a lot of what we see in action, both negative and positive, can be off-putting. Which makes it tricky to think about where we might fit into all of this – and how we might achieve 'good' or even 'great' as a speaker.

But speaking isn't something special, or something that only especially talented people can do – no, no, no, it's something we all should do, and can do. We all know how to talk, have a conversation, tell somebody something – why is it so terribly different when there's more than one person in front of you?

This chapter doesn't aim to furnish you with the definitive, and granular, 'how to do presentations and speaking'. There are dozens, if not hundreds, of well-written books on the subject and I recommend a few that have helped me at the end of the chapter.

What I will do is share my approach to starting a new talk – how to carve your big ideas into something coherent and interesting. I've got some pointers to help you go from 'yes, that was fine', to 'wow, fantastic job, thank you so much', regardless of where you speak or to whom. And I hope to get you thinking strategically about where you're going to open your mouth and say some stuff. Y'know, actually doing it for real.

Getting started

The question that most people come to me with when they want to become great speakers is 'Where do I start?' They might be working on a specific talk or keynote (a longer, conference style talk), or they may want to shake up existing material that goes along OK but could do with some va-va-voom.

The foundation for getting started is to work out *who* you want to speak to, and *why*. Only then can you begin to whittle down what you know into interesting pockets of content that your audience will be actually interested in. If you're an employee, it might be a case of asking yourself: 'Who do I *have* to talk to and why?'

BECKIE MADE HERSELF A LITTLE BIT FAMOUS, BY SPEAKING

The tech sector in the UK is experiencing a shortage of skilled people, as well as women leaders, so Beckie Taylor has stepped in to help plug the gap.

Having worked in tech herself, she runs continual training and coaching programmes for people who want to switch careers or get higher up the ladder. She shows them both the technical aspects and the personal skills you need for a career in tech.

Beckie made the decision to get out there more as a speaker on the subject in order to build her brand profile – and attract people to the work she does.

An ideal audience for Beckie would contain women who are juggling family commitments and want more flexible working hours, or who are looking for a new career or looking to progress within the industry.

Primarily she wants to fill her training programmes and make a difference to the tech industry. She wants her audiences to know that they can, and should, take advantage of great career opportunities.

RESULT: By sharing her experience and knowledge in this field, she has become known as a go-to expert on women in tech. She talks about the challenges of getting more women into the sector, and by offering her solution she finds that employers are increasingly coming to her to find women with the right skills in tech.

I asked Beckie what the overall impact of making herself a little bit famous, by speaking, has been:

'I find that I'm inspiring other women to enter tech by showing them it is possible. In their words, I have 'changed their lives'. If I can inspire them, and support them to enter the industry or progress to leadership positions, I feel that I'm making a big impact, which is hugely satisfying.'

Once you've settled on who your audience is and why you want/have to talk to them, then you're in a good place to get started on what you're going to say.

Your content is king

We tend to focus on performance when we think about speaking. How to stand, how to move our arms about. But that's like putting the cart before the horse. It's the content that's king here, and that's where the work is. Nerves dissipate and hand gestures become natural when you know your content is coherent and impactful.

I think of putting together a good talk, no matter what length, akin to producing a record. You wouldn't just bring along a bunch of ideas to the recording studio, would you? A rough notion as to how the drums, bass, lyrics, vocals and that other guitar will sound? You couldn't then record it all and try to sell the 'track' (or whatever it's called these days), because it would be utter crap.

It takes time to mix it all to make it sound good. There's a lot of creativity involved, which can be very rewarding, if you're prepared to dedicate some time to it. You've got to be the producer and the singer/songwriter for all the elements to hang together really well.

In big businesses, way too many presentations are driven solely by the information, omitting any creative 'production' of a talk. It would appear that slides are the most important bit, the thing that gets worked on first, and I can understand why. If you're presenting at a board-level meeting, it has to be accurate. If the slides are used as a handout, then some words and bullet points, graphs, etc. are useful, of course. The logos, language and style of the slides are the same across all presenters' decks, regardless of where they're speaking in the organisation.

But that can bog people down and prevent them from making a better fist of their delivery. The speakers end up wooden in their delivery and don't engage their audiences. And it becomes a benchmarked standard in the organisation that people fail to improve upon.

It's such a shame, as I can't begin to tell you the vast improvement I see in speakers when they are confident about their content – and that usually happens when they've allowed themselves, or have been allowed, to include something of themselves in it. And when you've got your content right, the potential for greatness is there.

In my humble opinion, the following elements are the cornerstones of super-dooper content that you will be proud to deliver:

- ▶ A strong message, or your overarching theme
- ▶ Stories and examples that underline your message and the points you want to make
- ▶ Solid structure, with signposting

(We could of course get all professional speakery on that, and turn the above into a 'model' of 'The Three S's'. Or how about 'The ESSSence of Speaking'? What fun!)

I'm happy once those elements are in place – everything else is a bonus. Only then can you focus on honing, shaping, improving and developing. But if you're up at the front of a room, or on a stage, fretting as to whether what you're saying makes any sense, or if it's boring or incoherent, then you're on a hiding to nothing.

And because no one likes a hiding to nothing, I'll go through them with you now. It's the process I use when I start building a talk, and one I use when helping clients.

Strong message

Finding your one message, or 'overarching umbrella theme', is very helpful, both in the planning and in the marketing of your talk. You may believe you've got loads of messages, but don't mix up 'your message' with your content, i.e. 'what you're going to actually say in your talk'.

Also, don't think about your company 'key messages' either – the corporate statements of 'what we are all about' – they're not that interesting. Audiences are WIFM-type people ('what's in it for me?').

Find your one message by asking yourself: what do you want your audience to know about?

One-word answers don't work. I have a keynote all about confidence, but I don't want my audiences to know about just confidence. I want them to know that confidence is an important and valuable foundation for life. And when individuals are confident in themselves, they make confident teams, and confident teams build better organisations. That's my angle on it; it's what I strongly believe in.

Interrogate the subject you want to talk about. For example:

- ► If leadership is your thing, then what is it specifically about leading that you want your audience to know about?
- ► If sales is your thing, what do you want your audience to know about sales, that you get excited about?
- ► If well-being is your thing, which bit of the whole world of

well-being do you want your audience to know about?

One of my speaker coaching clients, Rachel Haslam (no relation, although we share the fabulousness gene), is the owner of Team Academy, a business that works with organisations training teams and leaders. When I first asked her 'What do you want your audiences to know about?', she naturally said 'Teams!'

But delving deeper, we found her angle, which was the ability of team members to be vulnerable with each other, in order to trust each other. She wants audiences to know about the oft-overlooked importance of creating great teams that contribute to the success of their organisation. Only then were we able to set about finding stories and examples to fit that brief.

Clearly, if you have a new product or information about changes to your organisation then the scope for finding this overarching theme is limited. But it is still worth asking yourself the question, 'What do I want my audiences to know about and what do they want to hear about?', as it helps carve out the path to your message.

Five top tips for a strong message

▶ Get beneath the surface of your subject matter.
▶ Uncover the reason why you want to talk about it.
▶ What's *your* angle?
▶ Think about who you're speaking to and why.
▶ Your strong message is what helps sell your talk – so will it?

If you remember nothing else, remember this

No matter who your audience are, they will be WIFM people ('what's in it for me?').

Stories and examples

Stories and examples should *never* be left out of a talk or keynote – regardless of what you're talking about and to whom. I have tons of stories to tell, as you have probably realised, but that's not always been the case.

But since making speaking 'my thing' I see events, incidents and comments that happen in my everyday life as potential talk-fodder. I make a note of them, so I don't forget that hilarious thing my mum said the other day, etc. Most of the stories will never make it, but some of them are gems that you might use over the next ten years of your speaker journey.

For the listener, a story about a real-world, real-life example makes an impact. What would you rather hear about?

▶ Option A: a police report that says traffic is slowing to 10 mph on the anticlockwise lane of the city's ring road?

▶ Option B: a story about being stuck in a traffic jam on the A419 that makes you horribly late, and sweaty, for your dream job interview?

What's going to draw you in more, so you want to hear more? What's going to be remembered by the audience?

And for the performer, well-crafted stories are a pleasure to tell. I would urge you to use only stories you have experienced, rather than relaying an anecdote a mate told you. Or worse, sharing a well-known tale about a time so and so had dinner with the president, for example. And besides, when they're *your* stories, they're easy to remember. It's authentic and your audience is more likely to relate to you. Useful stuff when you're trying to land your message.

Describe the detail, offer the emotion

In your story, describe your surroundings and paint pictures with words. Describe the emotions and physical sensations you experienced at the time. Here's a transcript of one of my stories in a talk: what pictures does it paint, what emotions or physical sensations might you feel, if you were to hear it out loud?

My daughter Daisy and I were sitting on the sofa a few nights ago. [Picture]

She's 13 now, and so 'mum and daughter sitting on the sofa together' moments are getting rarer and rarer. [Emotion]

I had been looking through the newspaper and was showing her a black and white photograph of a woman, having run a race, with a number bib on her running shirt. [Picture]

The woman was just crossing a finishing line and had her hands raised above her head in absolute triumph. [Emotion]

She looked knackered, it has to be said. But then she had just done a lot of running. [Physical sensation]

The caption underneath the photograph said who she was: Fanny Blankers-Koen, the first and only woman to have won four athletics gold medals at a single Olympics, in London in 1948. Wow. [Emotion]

I read out the bit in the article to Daisy [picture] that told us that she had been nicknamed 'The Flying Housewife'. [Picture]

We paused to absorb the photograph and the impressive information about the athlete's achievements [picture and emotion] and then my daughter asked, in all honesty, 'What's a housewife?' [Emotion – if you think that's cool – it is though, isn't it?!]

Now, I could have said all of that in one sentence: my daughter doesn't know what a housewife is. End of.

But why would I miss an opportunity to press the imagination and emotions buttons on my audience? The impact of telling it like that is far greater than going for the factually accurate 'police report' sentence. So, give yourself permission to layer on more details – take us to the place, and share what you were thinking and feeling at the time.

And don't think for a minute that just because your audience is gathered for business information that they're not interested in you as a person. Even audiences that don't look like they're responding to your story will be. You are a human, speak in what humans really dig. Stories!

Selling from the stage, without being salesy

Another advantage of stories is that you can use them to 'sell in' what you do, what your business offers, or what your organisation's mission is. Of course, mention your credibility at some point during your talk, ideally near the beginning. It helps establish why you're the person who knows some stuff, and so we want to pay attention to what you're going to say.

But getting across what you sell, or what you do (or would like to do more of), can make us feel uncomfortable. If we brazenly start talking about our products or services, it feels like selling. And it is!

Instead, embed how you help people in the stories you tell. For example, I want to tell people that I work as a visibility coach, and the skills I teach in that are media skills, speaker skills and how to take part in panel discussions. I also want to make it known that I work with top teams and emerging leaders in large or medium-sized businesses.

So, which of these options would you prefer to hear as an audience member?

- ▶ Option A: 'Our confidence can sometimes escape us, can't it? And let me tell you, it doesn't matter how high up you are in your organisation. I was with a client last week who runs a national recruitment business, helping him work out how to take part in a panel discussion he's got coming up. He said to me: "Penny, it's daft I know, but who am I to be offering my expertise, when the other panellists have been working in the sector for much longer?"'
- ▶ Option B: 'I work as a visibility coach, helping top teams become brand ambassadors. You can talk to me afterwards to find out more, or go to my website. I'm competitively priced, but not the cheapest.'

Both say the same thing, but one is obvious and a turn-off, the other is a story and helps to subtly sell in what I do and place me as someone who can help.

Story arc

When I talk about story or narrative arcs, I feel very intelligent and artsy, so I've included this with pleasure.

That small vignette, a slice of life, of me and Daisy on the sofa learning about The Flying Housewife was a short story. It didn't take much crafting at the time. But you might have slightly longer tales to tell and those are best told along a classic story arc. This is a very basic spine of a story, but highly effective:

- ► Set the scene (the protagonists, the location)
- ► Indicate the emotion involved (was it scary, thrilling, disappointing)
- ► Highlight the conflict, jeopardy, the antagonist who comes along
- ► Darkest moment/biggest challenge to overcome
- ► Resolution/triumph

There are lots of story arc templates on the Internet that can help enormously.

Finding your stories

As I've suggested, keep your ears and eyes open for things that happen in your life, at home or through the work you do. Even the most mundane experience can be illuminating. Think about:

- ► your first day at school
- ► your first date or kiss
- ► the most embarrassing thing that ever happened to you
- ► a pet you owned
- ► your favourite teacher.

We've all got stories to tell, and they are most impactful when they are original and from your life. They don't have to be *about* you, but they should at least be original material and come from your world.

There's nothing worse than hearing a speaker tell a tale about someone they've never met, or something they read about in a book and are passing it off as their own. It's like a stand-up comedian telling an old joke that we are all familiar with and might even have told ourselves as some point, and expecting us to laugh.

Therefore the most obvious place to source your stories is from your world, isn't it? I was asked to speak in front of an audience of business travel bookers and I wanted to reflect their industry in my content. As I have little experience of having my business travel booked for me, I called up my cousin Fiona – who's never off a plane for her work.

I asked her about her recent travels and she told me about an illogical set of flight connections she'd been asked to make in order to save her company a few quid. It took away her much-needed recovery time, as she spent a Saturday night sitting round Delhi airport when she could have been relaxing at home watching *Strictly Come Dancing*.

No one else could tell this story, apart from Fiona, and as such I was telling my audience something they would not hear anywhere else. Through making the effort to interview her about her experiences, I was able to use her as the main protagonist in the story, which helped to illustrate the point I was making in my talk.

Five top tips for putting stories in your talk

▸ Listen out for stories from everyday life and make a note of them.

▸ Don't tell others' anecdotes and pass them off as your own.

▸ Re-live your story – perform it, don't just tell it.

▸ Paint pictures with words and add the emotions and physical sensations you experienced.

▸ Use a story arc where you can.

If you remember nothing else, remember this

You are the producer and the singer/songwriter – take control of it all, and make your talk a smash hit!

Solid structure, with signposting

If content is king, then structure is the queen. Without a solid structure, your talk will end up as an incoherent 'warm bath' for the recipient of your message. You might be perfectly good at performing on stage, or up at the front of the room, but you won't cut the mustard unless your structure is sound.

For structuring a good talk, step away from your computer. Do not write anything down in Word or open up PowerPoint in order to tinker with a bunch of slides that, as yet, have no home.

I'll get on to signposting in a bit, which is an important part of your structure. But let's kick off with what's going in our talks, and where it might fit.

This is where you can easily get your head in a muddle, and that's the danger if you start typing. So, here are a few things you could try to keep things clear in your head.

Affinity maps

I love an affinity map, they work every time – and it's an excuse to use my colourful Sharpie pens.

It's a way of finding ideas that seem to be related in some way, and putting them together. It helps me find the main themes of my content. It also prevents accidental repetition of an idea, or wedging in research or a story, that you're tempted to include.

Before I get into using Post-it notes and shuffling them about, I start with one big brain dump onto a piece of paper:

- ► Write down all the things you want to talk about – don't edit yourself, it's just a dumping ground.
- ► Then, get out your coloured pens and mark in different colours each thing that is similar. Or use several different shapes around each word or concept. These are your categories, or themes.
- ► Give those categories a title or name that references that 'chunk' of thinking.

Opposite is one I made earlier, when I was starting to drum up content for the travel industry keynote.

And you will find that *Sesame Street* can help here: if 'one of these things is not like the others, one of these things just doesn't belong' – it goes in the bin!

You end up with a handful of categories, or themes, which you can then swish across to a more structured, er, structure.

I used to love jigsaw puzzles when I was a kid, those big blocks that fit together to make a bright picture. Nothing fiddly or grown up like an image of a waterfall and thatched cottage for goodness' sake.

It's probably why I really love using this highly technical Post-it notes method, the affinity map, to order my thoughts and be able to see the emerging structure in front of me.

- ▶ Write out each idea from your big piece of paper on Post-it notes – your stories, facts, research, references.
- ▶ Discard any idea that doesn't naturally fit into a category.

- ▶ Then, group these under an appropriate title header.
- ▶ Order the Post-it notes vertically within each column, so they begin to make sense.
- ▶ Finally, put your columns, and the Post-its, in the order that you might talk about them.

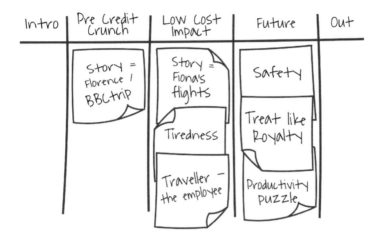

What, why and how

Once you've done the above, consider overlaying the what, why and how structure. I return to this time and time again and find most subjects lend themselves to this way of structuring what we need to say. Think about:

▶ **What** you are talking about: define your terms, say who it involves or affects, who benefits from hearing more about this. Essentially, setting out your stall.

▶ **Why** it is important: what do you lose out on if this isn't thought about, what's the jeopardy of doing/not doing this thing, or paying attention to this issue?

▶ **How** what you're talking about can be dealt with: can you offer a solution? You could suggest some action to take or a new way of thinking. Can you give your audience some practical 'take-homes' in order to do something differently?

You can use these three as your sections across the entire talk, if it's not too long – say, 15-20 minutes. Starting with what, then why and ending with how.

Or, for longer talks, around 45 minutes to an hour, you can use this structure within each of your categories or themes. Be careful not to overload each bit though, or you'll end up confusing your audience.

Writing it down

You've got your ideas into some semblance of order, the Post-its are in their columns, you've got your what-why-how ideas in there too – so now it's a case of refining every bit of it. At this point, I transfer my structure to a grid, on an A4 piece of paper, using a pencil and rubber.

I use the most brilliant planning grid on the planet, which was shown to me by the queen of presenting, Catherine Sandland (she is literally, on Twitter anyway, @presentingqueen).

Catherine and I met at the networking event where I'd first had a go at speaking about my business. She was about to start another of her six-monthly 'speaking clubs' in my area and I signed up immediately to learn how to get better.

I am very grateful to her for showing me this planning approach, as it appeals to my ordered and visual brain. I honestly didn't have a clue back then, but it's since become a mainstay for mapping out my content into a solid structure.

Opposite is one with 'instructions' for where to place your ideas on the grid. It's my tried and tested formula that I use for nearly all my talks, no matter how long or short.

INTRO (WHAT ARE YOU TALKING ABOUT, WHY YOU, WHY THEY SHOULD LISTEN)	CHUNK 1 (WHAT IT IS)	CHUNK 2 (WHY IT IS IMPORTANT)	CHUNK 3 (HOW IT CAN BE SOLVED, WHAT YOU NEED TO THINK ABOUT/DO)	OUT
Hello! **I'm going to talk about...** **It's important because...** **You will learn...** **I'm passionate and credible because...** **You might be someone who...** **(list 3 max audience member scenarios for whom this might help)...**	**And first of all, it's important to understand what we're dealing with... so what I'm going to tell you is:** *The scenario as it is now* *The scenario as it could be* *A story* *Some facts* *A slide with image on it.* *Jeopardy: what if we ignore this?*	**What I'm going to tell you about is:** *The scenario as it is now* *The scenario as it could be* *A story* *Some facts* *A slide with image on it?* *Jeopardy: what if we ignore this?*	**What I'm going to tell you about is:** *The scenario as it is now* *The scenario as it could be* *A story* *Some facts* *A slide with image on it?* *Jeopardy: what if we don't take action?*	**And what all of that means, is that you now know what to...** *Feel (recap)* *Know (recap)* *Do (recap)* **Embedding Q&A: Before I finish up, we've got time for a couple of questions...**
What I'm going to show you is going to help...	*What I've just told you is...*	*What I've just told you is...*	*What I've just told you is...*	*Thank you for those questions, wrap up with rallying call to action finale:* E.g. "If we all talk in the same way, we can be a really strong and powerful voice for social change." **Thank you!**

You can get your own blank one-sheet planner from the website **makeyourselfalittlebitfamous.com**

It's a bit like a map of a journey, with a start and end point, all on one sheet of paper. What happens in between is easy to see at a glance.

The other option of course is to type out your content, everything that you're going to say, page after page. It might be how you've approached it in the past, and might work for you. The problem with that is you will end up with a script and won't have the 'overview' that the planner gives you.

Through working on my structure and placing the elements of my content into the columns, I become really familiar with the order of what I'm going to say.

I don't go for perfection on the first sheet I use, either – I'll get through several sheets in the course of mapping out my talks. Over time, the amount of information or words in each column reduces because, as I've gone along, I've said it out loud and have got to know the stories and idea, and can articulate them more fluently each time. Eventually, I'm down to just bullet points noted in each of the columns.

Remembering it all – is it even possible?

I think it is so cool when you can walk around a stage with your entire talk in your head. It is so freeing. For me, the one-sheet planner is my friend on the day, as well as being a useful tool in my prep.

And, don't tell anyone, but I sometimes take it on stage with me, like a child's comfort blanket. Or, if I was actually cool, my set list! Audiences don't notice it, and don't care, if I leave it on the lectern, or pop it on the floor in front of me. I rarely look at it, but I know it's there. Comforting or what?

If you don't yet trust the one-sheet planner, are prone to brain freeze, or worry you'll forget where you are in your talk, then use cue cards or notes. But whatever you do, don't use a script. It will prohibit you from knowing, at a glance, what's coming up because it's written over several A4 pages. Every page turn will bring you a surprise. And most people are not skilled in the art of writing for speech, so it will make you sound wooden or formal, when you really don't want to be that, do you?

Signposting

Signposting, or transitioning, from one topic to the next is overlooked by many speakers. I've been guilty of it in the past, which is why I am now very thorough in practising these junctions in my talks. They're very important, as they help the audience know where they are in your talk. Like a chapter in a book coming to an end, and a new chapter title being announced on a fresh page.

The junctions I'm talking about come at the end of a section of information, stories and ideas. Those sections are likely to follow along the lines of your categories.

Approach it by thinking along the lines of 'I want the audience to know we're parking that first concept, and that I'm about to share a new thought with them' – so how might you do that?

The classic rule of thumb for actually articulating these transitions is:

'Tell them what you're going to tell them, tell them, then tell them what you've just told them.'

Starting a fresh idea can be indicated really well through non-verbal communication too. You could move to a different bit of the stage, pause, and/or chuck in some 'starter sentences', such as:

► 'So, next, I'm going to talk about...'
► 'Now, if you thought that was a good idea, I'm going to tell you about another important bit of thinking...'
► 'Before I finish, I've got one last thought to share with you...'

And repeat this every time you move on to a new big chunky idea. No wonder we forget about this important element of our structure; it's so laborious! But it works, and as boring and repetitive as you feel it is, it's worth doing well. Your audience will thank you for it.

Five top tips for structuring your talk

► Dump all of your thinking onto a big piece of paper, get a sense of what goes with what and then swish those ideas across to Post-it notes.
► Separate out the different categories of your subject into columns.
► Create space in your talk for signposting, telling the audience what's happening.
► Keep all of your one-sheet planners in a plastic wallet folder, for future reference.
► Use Sharpies, they are the lifeblood of structures.

If you remember nothing else, remember this

Say more about less – don't overcomplicate the structure of your content.

Going for gold – from good to great as a speaker

All of this chapter so far, will stand you in good stead for talks or delivering speeches. With what you've learned so far, you should be able to communicate your message with clarity, in a solid structure, and pull off a good performance.

Get as much experience under your belt as you can and your abilities will improve, there's no doubt about that.

However, there are a few extra things you can do that will help you go from good to great as a speaker.

Your introduction – don't leave it to chance

Ahead of speaking at an event, it's customary to send some information about yourself to the event organiser, along with a high-resolution photograph, to help with their marketing.

It's usually a 50-100 word biog, or a copy and paste of the 'meet the team' blurb from your own website, that they use on the event website, in the flyers they put out on chairs, or in the conference brochure.

That's all good – but it's also what gets sent to the event host, or moderator, if there is one. They typically receive a list of who is going to be speaking, along with your biog.

The problem is that an inexperienced host might not think to rewrite the information she/he's been sent about you – and then just read it out loud.

There are three reasons why this is bad:

1. It is bound to be way too long and will eat into discussion time.
2. It is a repeat of the website/flyer/brochure blurb and so isn't adding value for the audience.

3. It has been written to be read, not written to be spoken – thus inviting stumbles and monotone delivery.

An answer to all of this pain is to say that you are the best person to write your introduction. Or you are at the mercy of the organiser, and whether the chair has enough time to rewrite your biog (and make a good job of it).

As well as including information about you, your intro is a chance to tee-up what you're going to talk about. You can whet the audience's appetite for knowing more.

Your introduction should include:

► who you are
► what you do
► a small amount of relevant background – if there's none, so be it
► what you're going to talk about
► why it's relevant to the audience.

A big thank you to Jeremy Nicholas, my Professional Speaking Association mate and fellow event host, for the origination of this pithy formula. He says, and I wholly concur, that the skeleton of your introduction works best when laid out like this:

'Our next speaker is *your job title and organisation.** S/he is focused on *something or other** at the moment, and has worked for a range of/has experience of *some other things.**

S/he is passionate about *so and so,** and is now going to share how she/he overcame the challenge of *that thing you're going to talk about.**

Please welcome your name here!*'
(*delete/edit as appropriate)

Then you smile, walk on to rapturous applause, smug in the knowledge your introduction has injected some energy and useful information before you've even opened your mouth. Also, your name is more likely to be remembered if it is heard just before you walk on, rather than at the beginning of the intro.

Most importantly, write it to be spoken. Try it yourself, out loud, to see if it scans well or if certain words make you stumble.

And as tempting as it seems, do *not* include your gap year in that difficult to pronounce city in Romania, all the charity and school boards you're on, the 10Ks you've run... and so on. The audience is not interested and, besides, they may well have read about all of that in the event literature already.

This is one I wrote for a speaker I was introducing at a National Housing Federation event (a room full of ambitious, forward-thinking, social housing communications professionals):

Our next speaker is the exec director of Climate Outreach, and specialises in communicating the issues of climate change to the widest possible audiences.

Today he's going to talk about the lessons they learned on audiences that are traditionally seen as being hostile to the climate change issue. So you can use them in your communication about social housing.

Please welcome Jamie Clarke...

Email your introduction to the organiser and the person introducing you, well in advance. And, belt and braces, bring a paper copy, printed in large font, in case they're a bit amateurish and have forgotten about it.

Top tip: Keep it snappy.

Get a grip on nerves

Nerves and adrenaline can hamper your performance. They can place you on an emotional rollercoaster for a few days which, despite its name, isn't much fun.

Until I got a grip on my nerves I felt exhausted after delivering a talk or chairing a conference. It was the build-up, the preparation and the effort on the day that had my adrenaline pumping – sometimes for weeks in advance. As a result, I was wiped out for a good couple of days afterwards.

When I finally got my head around the idea that preparation isn't just about the technical aspects of talking, things started to change for me. I'm calmer, more confident, more present in the moment so I can enjoy it all a bit more.

In the days leading up to an event, I use breathing techniques, and positive visualisation (all discoverable on the Internet). I drink loads of water before, during and after, and get as much sleep as I can. All of that has really helped me, so give it a whirl.

Mental and physical prep for you as a person is a major part of giving a great performance. Athletes don't stroll on up for a 100-metre sprint having just been down the car wash or supermarket, do they? So why would you be able to hop up onto a stage, as though it's nothing?

Top tip: Think about what you can do to help yourself be a better performer. What is in your pre-speaking 'routine'?

Abolish negative self-talk

The way in which you talk to yourself (self-talk) is very important in life in general – but even more so when you're under pressure to deliver a talk or speech. I have heard so many people say, out loud:

- ► 'It's all going to go horribly wrong.'
- ► 'I'm going to be shit.'
- ► 'They [the audience] will be bored.'
- ► 'I think I'll call in sick.'

Imagine what they say to themselves, inside their heads!? And it's not weird or unusual because we all say stuff to ourselves that is critical or foretells doom and gloom. We wouldn't dream of speaking to others the way we sometimes talk to ourselves, would we?

So, if you've got a propensity for damaging negative self-talk, and want to improve and maybe enjoy speaking, then you simply have to change the script inside your head. Talk to yourself in an encouraging way! It is the key to getting out from under the stinky and heavy rock of self-doubt and uncertainty about your abilities.

Try these as replacements when you're being negative or nasty to yourself:

- ► 'I am very smiley when I first start speaking and people really like that.'
- ► 'I know exactly what I'm talking about, this is my project after all.'
- ► 'I'm going to be so relaxed when I walk onto the stage.'

Top tip: Note any positive remarks that people have made to you after you've spoken, or during your preparation. And repeat them to yourself, a lot. Let them puff up your chest, you beautiful person you.

SLOW down

One common problem I see when I'm training people in their speaking performance is that they speak too quickly because they're nervous. Speak too fast and you get your words muddled – you can leave sentences unfinished and get in a brain tangle (a brangle?) with yourself. Ultimately, you don't land your point well and you can't guarantee you've been understood.

You've gone to the effort of preparing your content, perfecting your slides and running a brush through your hair, so make the effort to communicate clearly.

Recently, I was encouraged by the authorities to attend a Speed Awareness Course (don't judge me, it was late, I didn't know the area, etc...). The instructor told us that whenever we see the white painted sign in the road 'SLOW', think of it as 'Speed Low, Observe Well'. And I do, every flipping time!

I have doctored that phrase slightly, useful for when you're on stage and getting into top-gear gum-flapping. Think of me in your ear, whispering 'Speed Low, Offer Wisdom'.

Which sage-sounding person ever garbled their words?

Top tip: Make a conscious effort to slow down if you know you're guilty of being a bit of a fast talker.

Energy and pace

Hands up who likes a lacklustre speaker? No one, that's who. Lacklustre is a result of a lack of energy and pace in delivery style. But don't confuse slowing down the speed at which you speak with reducing the energy you bring to your performance.

Your talk should have an engaging and energised pace, and you can ensure this by giving your topics the time they deserve. And no more. What I'm saying is, don't go on.

Remember the analogy about making a record? You can't really tell if you have too much of one thing, or not enough of another, unless you rehearse it, ideally in front of others. Time your sections, and make sure there's balance. Eliminate the draggy bits and you will travel through your talk with pace.

If you are a very confident speaker, and it suits your style, you will be able to speak fairly quickly, and be understood. This injects energy and pace too, of course. The comedian Dave Gorman delivers his material at top speed, but he is word perfect, well rehearsed and you don't miss a thing.

Top tip: Enthuse, be punchy and upbeat! Life's dreary enough as it is, don't be a dreary speaker.

Humour in your talk

Please be funny. Audiences are crying out to be entertained. We need more fun in the world – don't we? That doesn't mean you should become an after-dinner speaker or stand-up comedian. Nor should you dumb down how you explain things.

But injecting some laughs into what you say will help your audience remember what you're saying even more.

You could:

- Smile.
- Be humorous early on, so your audience know that it's OK to laugh when you say something funny.
- Steal the tricks that stand-up comedians use in their sets, it gives the impression you're a very confident performer too. They are:
  - Saying hello to the audience when you first come on.
  - Chuckling at your own jokes.
  - Telling 'asides' halfway through telling a story.
- Acting out stuff.
- Use funny slides – pictures of you as child in a daft outfit, for example.
- Have a notebook for relevant or funny stories you hear in the course of your everyday life.
- Be self-deprecating, but not to the point of running yourself down.
- Don't be funny at others' expense or poke fun at an audience member.
- Don't tell jokes. Most people are terrible at telling jokes.

Top tip: Embrace your funny bone! Own it!

Getting feedback

When I was first on the BBC's *Breakfast* programme, presenting the business news, with all the bright lights and cameras, I found it difficult to gauge whether or not I had done a good job. I was often highly self-critical, as we can be, and wasn't in the right frame of mind to give myself an objective, let alone positive, view of my performance.

The same applies for most people about speaking in public, either at meetings or on a stage. They say, '... it went OK. But I was so nervous.'

And then they'll tell me about one thing that went wrong, or an audience member who looked at their phone the whole time.

Then, after they've finished focusing on how they felt about it and their perceived negatives, they might pluck up the courage to ask others what they thought. Anyone watching would probably say, regardless of the truth, that 'it was fine'.

Fine? Fine! There's nothing worse! We really, deep down, want a constructive and well-thought-through answer to this question:

'Was-I-crap-and-how-can-I-be-better? Or-was-it-really-rather-impressive-and-you're-blown-away?'

If you want feedback, ask in advance and brief your colleague or friend specifically on what you want them to look and listen out for.

I also suggest you video your talk on your phone – either get someone to hold it on the front row, or get a stand for it and place it near you so it picks up the sound. Review it after your adrenalised self-critic has stepped down and you'll be in a better place to weigh up what went well and what you can do better. This will also capture turns of phrase you said at the time that worked really well and you might want to use again.

You be the judge. You decide. Get into self-critiquing with kindness.

Top tip: Feedback is like a gift. You don't have to like it and can always shove it somewhere and jog on with your life.

How to get on stages in the first place

If you can, think strategically about your speaking activity. Go back to *why* you want to speak, and *who* needs to hear you. And then make a plan, list what you need to do in order to gain the skills you need and set a goal for the number of times you want to speak.

It takes time to get booked into conferences and events, and get known as someone who speaks. But getting as many on-stage hours under your belt as possible will help you improve enormously.

Here are some tips about how to get on stages in the first place:

▶ Ask to speak! Contact event organisers or association leads – suggest yourself as a speaker at their next event.

▶ Keep a calendar of events. If you get email invitations to events, announcing speakers, then it's likely they'll have another event in the future. Make a note, and get in touch – as early as six months ahead.

▶ Tell the people around you that you want to speak. Have a word with your boss, and say that you want to represent your company externally, or do more presentations.

▶ If you work somewhere with a press office or marketing department, make friends there and tell them you'd be keen to 'get out there' on behalf of the brand.

▶ Use your contacts, think about who you know who speaks and ask them for ideas.

▶ Speak for free or go pro. Or a mixture of both. Most professional speakers I know do occasional freebies, when the audience might be full of potential customers for their training or it could lead to more speaking opportunities. If you're starting out, then get as many on-stage opportunities as possible in order to hone your craft and get better.

▶ If you're already speaking, either delivering talks and keynotes, or training and coaching, join an association. The Professional Speaking Association (PSA) is for speakers, trainers and coaches who speak for a living, or aspire to. The motto is 'Speak More – Speak Better'. Which has always struck me as slightly grammatically incorrect – but it certainly does what it says on the tin. I've been a member for nearly five years and it has played a huge part in my success. The PSA has regional groups across the UK, and is part of the Global Speakers' Federation.

▶ For performance skills and stagecraft, try a 'speaking club' such as Toastmasters or Speakers' Express in London. You'll get front-of-room experience straight away and feedback on your performance style.

▶ Run your own event. You could put on your own, or deliver a breakfast seminar at your place of work for clients.

▶ TEDx talks. Great for kudos, and for the video they take of you. Make sure your idea is actually worth spreading, and that you incorporate something relevant for the location in which it is being held.

Want more? Read these:

▶ *Executive Presentations* by **Jacqui Harper.** No stone is unturned in this brilliant guide to speaking – there's content, structure, style, performance, even what to wear.

▶ *The Art of Plain Speaking: How to Write and Speak in a Way that Will Impress the People that Matter* by **Charlie Corbett.** This was the winner of the Short Business Book of the Year at the Business Book Awards, 2019.

▶ *How to Deliver a TED Talk: Secrets of the World's Most Inspiring Presentations* by **Jeremey Donovan.** Jeremey spells his name a bit oddly, but his book is great for any talk, not just TED talks.

chapter 5

MAKE YOURSELF A LITTLE BIT FAMOUS... ON PANELS

My father used to say, 'Don't raise your voice; improve your argument.'

Desmond Tutu

Panels are the bread and butter of most gatherings where information is shared. Either as stand-alone events in themselves, or as an element of a longer conference or summit.

It's a chance for a variety of industry or sector-related individuals to come together and chew over a few ideas that the audience may find interesting and of use to them.

Ideally the panellists are knowledgeable, experienced and passionate about the subject area and have something interesting to say.

They can also be deathly dull and turn audiences right off. You know the ones, where you wish you were at home rearranging your sock drawer.

Wouldn't it be great if everyone on a panel took responsibility for putting on a great 'show'? And then, as a result of that effort, wouldn't it be just dreamy if those people were liked and remembered more by the people in the audience?

I've met lots of different panellists and their various attitudes and approaches to the task in hand. There are people who are diligent and keen to do a great job; others, for whatever reason, fail to prepare anything decent to say, thinking they can wing it.

I recently chaired a panel that dealt with helping businesses and postgraduates find each other and work together. One of the panellists avoided me like the plague before the start of the panel, during the registration and coffee bit, when I was due to meet and greet those taking part. He'd also not replied to my emails that week, so I had not been able to establish much about him or what his angle would be during the discussion.

The overall impression I got from his behaviour was that he was standoffish and aloof. Actually, reading between the lines, he was nervous and felt out of his depth.

Because of his lack of communication with me, creating a situation where I couldn't support and help him, he left himself wide open. He didn't know what topics were coming up, so hadn't prepared anything.

As a result, he had naff all to say that was of any interest. I ended up asking the panellists who were doing a better job of it in the discussion. He missed an opportunity to shine, didn't he?

So, this chapter focuses on your performance on a panel, whether you're a panellist or tasked with chairing it.

What does good look like?

As a professional panel chair, my dream panel discussion is lively, energetic, inspiring, interesting and useful. Why? Apart from stopping me snoozing off while I'm pretending to be interested in what you're saying, it's actually in my blood after 20 years at the BBC and being responsible for putting on a jolly good show.

During my time as a senior producer on BBC Radio 4, I regularly pulled together stimulating debate for round-table discussion programmes. I dealt with dry or seemingly niche subject matters. I sourced the right expert guests to take part, who had something to say but didn't overlap in their experiences.

I structured the airtime to pay attention to the important stuff that would be of interest to our audience; but not to make it so overstuffed with content that the topics and the guests couldn't chew them over.

I want the Reithian BBC values to come to life. To educate, inform and entertain – *wherever* there is an audience.

Why you should say yes, and why people say no

Saying yes to being part of a panel discussion is another clever way to shake hands with the whole room in one go – the audience gets to hear about what you do, your business, what you stand for and how you help people.

You can easily raise your professional standing, that of your business, brand, or product, by appearing on a panel or chairing one. And if your performance is good, you'll be memorable, likeable – and might make a business connection with someone in the audience, if not immediately, then later down the line.

That's the theory anyway, and intellectually we can follow that logic. Emotionally, however, we might have a different response: a basic instinct that tells us to run for the hills.

I was at an event speaking to an audience of business owners and employees who wanted to know more about 'getting out there'. I was delivering my Make Yourself a Little Bit Famous talk to give them ideas and inspiration to raise their profile.

I was chatting to a finance director called Isabelle at the teas, coffees and selection of old-school biscuits table. She told me that my talk was extremely timely, as she'd just agreed to be a panellist at an industry event next month and she'd never done anything like it before.

I was just about to congratulate her for doing the very thing I bang on about all the time when she told me she was thinking of cancelling! She wasn't sure what to expect and was worried she'd not be able to get her points across well enough.

And this is a fairly typical response. Many people will say no straight away for those very reasons, or they say yes and get tangled up with nerves and uncertainty about their performance.

But like most things, as soon as we get some practical experience and guidance under our belt, our concerns vanish. We might even find ourselves enjoying being part of a team of people who are essentially having a chat about stuff they know about.

Hats off to Isabelle though, she bit the bullet and went on that panel, because by the end of my talk she was in no doubt that it's one of the best ways to get exposure for what you do.

Techniques for panellists

There is scant information about how to be a great panellist – no one hands you a guide on how to do it. Apart from me, right now, of course.

And there's no good reason why you shouldn't stand out in your performance. Frankly, the bar is set pretty low so it doesn't take much to look really good.

My hope is that you ultimately enjoy the experience of taking part in a panel discussion, once you've got the following in your brain…

How much time do you get?

Working out how much time you have in which to speak is crucial – so you know how much you can say, which in turn impacts on your preparation. There's no point preparing yards of information if you've only got a couple of minutes to say it.

Knowing the amount of 'airtime' you have also helps keep you on point, so you can make an impact right away and ditch extraneous words/sentences. During my time as a panel chair, I've heard a lot of this sort of padding/waffle:

'... it's great to be here. I was coming here tonight thinking about what we all need to be thinking about and we've got a lot of challenges ahead but the issues really are, as I see them, well, a bit similar to the first speaker, who said...', etc.

All of which are a waste of your own time. So, jump in with, 'my point on this would be...' and then make it.

How to work out your 'airtime'

If the discussion is billed as a 30-minute slot in total, and you know you'll be sharing that time with three other panellists, plus a panel chair who's got to do intros and ask the questions (so that's five of you), then you have approximately six minutes' speaking time. Not that long is it?

Audience Q&A might be in addition to that time or part of it, but find out exactly what the structure is beforehand so you're forewarned.

Top tip: Don't waste your own airtime. Eliminate waffle and get straight to your point, saying your best stuff first (in case you don't get the chance again).

Your introduction

How you get introduced on the day is important, and it doesn't matter who does it. It might be down to the panel chair to do it, or they might ask you to say a few words about who you are and what you think about the panel discussion theme.

Just as in speaking at an event, I suggest you take control over this one and write your own introduction. See page 93 for how to do this really well.

Topics for discussion

In an ideal world, the chair, or at least the event organiser, will have been in touch to give you the context for the panel discussion. It's good to know if it's part of a wider conference or is the main attraction of the event.

They should also be able to tell you in some detail (and if they don't, then ask about the following well in advance):

- ▶ The theme of the event.
- ▶ The title of the panel discussion.
- ▶ The topics or angles they want to cover.
- ▶ Who is in the audience: generally, what do they do and what level are they.

They might also invite you to add ideas of your own.

In an ideal world, you'd have a conference call or even a face-to-face meeting with everyone on the panel ahead of the actual event. It builds rapport and certainly makes for a much better discussion.

Do enquire about this and see if it's possible, especially so the panel chair understands more about what you've got to say, so can ask you about that on the day.

But most event organisers and panel chairs don't consider this a priority – they're time poor and have a million other more important things to do, so don't be surprised if this isn't arranged.

If that's not possible, email communication has to suffice and you do your best with that.

Once you've got the general areas for discussion, prepare some interesting stuff to say on each. The more bespoke, personal and relevant to the audience, the better. It's as simple as that.

Expect the unexpected: the conversation may take a different direction to the one you've prepared for; time may not allow for everything to get covered; or you may find yourself with a time-dominator panellist who leaves you with little time to say your best stuff.

A word of warning if you're asked to take part in a discussion about an 'issue' – for example, women on boards, improving education, care of the elderly, mental health in the workplace – as there's a tendency for them to become talking shops. Where real life, practical examples, are in short supply. You'll hear phrases such as:

'We ought to be doing this that or the other, because our industry is focusing on this, that and the other and what's important is that we continue to strive towards...'

Blah, blah. Boring! So although the sentiment might be passionate, the actual words you end up ushering may be of no use to the audience whatsoever.

Of course, take the discussion seriously but don't forget it's your job to educate, inform and entertain your audience! Be charming and above all be helpful – include plenty of practical examples (use FACE in chapter 3 to nail this).

Top tip: Prepare some interesting stuff to say and say it sooner rather than later.

Expand the conversation

Don't just sit quietly waiting to be asked a question by the chair. Jump in to the conversation and add to the point that's being made. This brings energy and a liveliness that can really hold an audience's attention.

But don't interrupt someone else's point while they're making it – that's just rude whether you're on a panel or not. **Top tip:** Think dinner party discussion, not job interview.

Energy and rapport

Adrenaline and nerves can wreak havoc on your energy levels. You may experience a dip about halfway through when your fight-or-flight hormones settle down and you realise you're not going to die as a result of being on a panel. Sluggish panellists make for soporific events.

Even if you're not 'feeling it', then manufacture rapport with the other panellists, the chair and the audience. Be yourself on a good day and look interested in what others are saying.

Looking at your nails/watch, texting or picking fluff off your lapels gives the impression that you'd rather be somewhere else, so check your body language and facial expression if you're prone to this sort of thing.

Enthusiastic and active participants are far more likeable and memorable.

Check in on yourself during the discussion. Take a deep breath, sit up straight, smile and focus.

You'll know if you've got it right when you look out at the audience. If all you see is the tops of people's heads, then they are checking their emails or shopping online. Sure, go ahead, tell yourself they're tweeting your latest pearl of wisdom…

Top tip: An engaged audience wants eye contact and to spend more time looking at you and your fellow panellists than they do at their phones.

Where do you look?

Who should you be looking at when you're up at the front of the room taking part in a panel? The audience? The other panellists? The chair of the panel?

The natural position is to only look at your peers and the panel chair when you're talking – the others who are taking part in the discussion. But a good panellist will make the effort to look at the audience. It will make them feel included, and you can connect with them far more than if you only make eye contact with the panel.

Top tip: Make eye contact with one or two audience members straight away, and smile.

Remembering the question

Daft as it may sound, one of the strangest and most unexpected experiences for panellists is when the chair looks at you and asks you, 'So what do *you* think about that?'... *and you've forgotten the original question!* It's the stuff of anxiety dreams for sure.

How could you forget the question? Hey, it's easily done, and for a couple of reasons when you're on a panel.

One, is that nerves and adrenaline can hamper our thought processes; and two, there might have been one, two, or even three people's answers before you get your turn.

With practice, you can hold the question in your mind, or at least a rough idea of it.

It's perfectly acceptable to have a notebook with you when

you're taking part in a panel, so use it to jot down a word or two that will help you remember the original question. Or anything you think of along the way while others are talking. **Top tip:** If you *do* lose the plot, then just admit it, make a joke of it – it's not a crime. Don't sit there struggling – someone will happily remind you what the talking point is.

Dealing with audience questions

Nearly every panel discussion will include a decent amount of time for audience questions, much more than if you were speaking. It's facilitated by the panel chair, so you don't need to 'do' anything, other than pay attention to the questions and answer them if you can.

It sounds straightforward enough, but there can be some curveballs to deal with. Here are a few different audience Q&A scenarios you will come across:

- ▶ Audience members sometimes offer comments that go on a bit, rather than ask questions. They often start by saying 'This is more of a comment than a question…' at which point everyone in the room rolls their eyes.
- ▶ Audience members can ask long questions, or a series of questions. If it falls to you to answer, sum up and then take the questions one at a time. Or, do what most people do, and answer the bit you can remember (usually the last bit) and then jog on.
- ▶ The chair might come to you for a response to one of the questions posed, but you might not have the answer. In that case, you could:
  - ▷ Bridge on to what you *can* talk about: 'Well I don't

know about that, but a similar situation came up for
me when...'

▷ Pass the buck, kindly: 'That's not my area of expertise,
I'd have thought Asma would know far more than I
do...' (Then hopefully Asma answers the question!)

▶ The question might require a huge amount of detail that
would be of no interest to the rest of the audience. Offer
to talk to them later, or invite them to email you.

▶ Say you'll be sticking around after the discussion for the
drinks/networking bit – if anyone wants to talk to you,
you'd be more than happy to take their questions, etc. (and
then don't run off after you're done – it's an opportunity to
meet your new fans and gather connections).

Top tip: Your answers to audience questions are another
opportunity to use FACE (chapter 3), which provides useful
content and will be more memorable to the audience.

Be bang up to date

Don't live in a news bubble. If you're going to get exposure for
what you do, you simply can't hide from this one – whether it's
panels you're doing or anything else. Sounding out of date, or
just being out of the loop of what's going on in the world in
terms of trends and issues, is not a good look.

I'm staggered at the number of people who say they want to
'get out there' yet say they don't pay attention to the news – be
it 'the news' or latest industry stuff. C'mon, get yourself updated!

This is especially important in the lead-up time to your
panel appearance, and on the day of the event itself. You
should apprise yourself of the latest industry issues – no doubt

you do this anyway – but you should also know what's going on in the news generally.

For industry or panel theme-related news you could reflect on the latest information and sound super expert as a result. For example, if you're discussing investments and the markets have just wobbled about a bit, then have a bit of that info up your sleeve.

If you're the only one in the room who doesn't know about something major and it simply cannot be ignored by the panel chair, then you're going to look and feel a bit daft. We're talking here about the big deal stuff, royal death, presidential assassination, etc.

So, before the event, on the way there, or just before heading up onto the stage, it makes sense to check trusted news sources. The reason for saying 'trusted' is that I hear a lot of panellists attempting to recall where they saw something.

'Er, I think I saw on Facebook, or was it Insta, last month I think, that said...'

The rule of thumb: don't do this. And if you do, don't cite anything but trusted sources in your panel conversation as it can destroy your credibility in an instant. If you use my FACE in your preparation you will have citations front of mind anyway, so you will avoid this hazard.

Top tip: Do not rely on social media feeds or 'news' outlets/ blogs (unless they link to one of those trustworthy sources).

By now, you'll have some seriously practical tips and techniques for being amazing on panels. I hope you'll go on to thoroughly enjoy taking part in these types of discussions and benefit from the exposure they give you.

ROWENA MADE HERSELF A LITTLE BIT FAMOUS... ON A PANEL

My pal Rowena Birch is a judo Olympian (I know! I'm mates with an Olympian!!), European champion and England judo coach.

She asked for my help ahead of going on a panel at an event at Manchester University, where she wanted to influence and inform their thinking about sport and study. In the audience were not only students, but important financial decision makers.

She was apprehensive about being involved and, as the only person with a professional sporting background, she was putting a lot of pressure on herself. I told her what I've just told you in this chapter, about what to bear in mind when you're up on the stage or the front of the room, being expert and wonderful.

She reported back that it went really well. As a result of knowing what to expect and how to make her points well, she felt like she'd won another medal! She rang me from her car on the way home, well chuffed with herself:

'It was amazing and I really held my own, jumping into the discussion and moving it on! By the end, I was holding the room with my story examples and passion for sport at university – plus my call to action. Without your help, I'd not have felt it was my place to be like that. I played big as a result.'

About 18 months after her first panel appearance, Rowena told me that additional funding for sport had been granted at the university. I daresay she had helped that along, having raised awareness of the value of sport in front of those key decision makers.

She also said she'd grown in confidence, so when she was invited to take part in a panel discussion for International Women's Day, 'Celebrating Inspiring Women in Manchester', she had no problem saying 'Yes!' straight away.

Rowena built on her experience as a panellist when she was asked to chair a panel at another event soon afterwards. She told me:

'I had lots of great feedback afterwards and I don't think anyone guessed it was my first time in this role.'

The lesson here is, the more you do, the more you *can* do. And when you do 'get out there', you might also be effecting change.

Five top tips for being a brilliant panellist

▶ Smile, breathe, keep your energy up.

▶ Jump into discussion, but don't interrupt.

▶ Look interested when others are speaking.

▶ Be aware of turn-taking in the conversation – don't dominate it, or say too little.

▶ Be bang up to date.

If you remember nothing else, remember this

Bring your comments to life with real-world stories – use FACE in chapter 3 to prepare your thoughts, and the points you want to make, before the event.

Techniques for panel chairs

Without a 'chair' for your panel, a panel discussion is just a nice, rangy, conversation. A bit directionless and leaderless.

So, nearly all discussions require someone to host the party. This is not a small ask, it's a *big* ask. If I were to generalise, event organisers tend to play down just how big a job this is, perhaps because they've not done it themselves or they believe it will 'just happen'.

By the way, I'm going to use the word 'chair' as opposed to moderator, facilitator or host. It doesn't matter which of those words you choose to describe this role, it basically means the person who asks the questions, ensures the panellists don't guff on for too long and (with luck) brings the proceedings to a close on time.

Chairing a panel is one of my favourite types of work as a professional speaker because I consider it a privilege to ask people interesting questions. And it's a pleasure to host what I consider to be my very own BBC Radio 4-style 'round table' discussion in front of a live audience.

I use techniques from journalism to think up great questions and probe for better answers. And direct the themes so the audience gets what they came for. I like to introduce humour too, because all too often these things are dry as hell.

This role, with its many titles, is what you make it and there are a number of reasons why you might find yourself in this particular hot seat:

▶ Your boss was meant to do it, but now can't be bothered, so has 'asked' you to do it.

▶ You're a sponsor at the event, or in some way involved,

and the organiser needs to give you something to do, so you get recognition.

► You're the MC of the event and it's part of your remit.

So, yes, you can stumble onto stage, do very little and probably get by, or you can see it as 'your show' to run in the way you like.

Whatever the circumstances for finding yourself as the person asking the questions and driving the discussion, I would recommend you take it seriously and *own it*!

Why? Well, it's an opportunity to shine, stand out, be seen as credible, kick-ass and authoritative. And the reason you've got the role is because people think you're up to it. This section will give you the full job description, with tips and techniques.

Although you're the person asking the questions there are opportunities to input with your own knowledge, experience and passion too – this is really welcomed by audiences, because they love it when you've got intelligent things to say and therefore aren't just chopped meat with a list of questions to get through.

A lot of panel chairs throw away this opportunity because they forget to take ownership of it.

Let's take a look at the job description and make sure that doesn't happen for you. It's based on my years of experience at the coalface of panel chairing. Here's my long list of everything you are responsible for:

► liaising with the event organiser and panellists
► helping to decide themes and interesting areas for discussion, based on the panellists' areas of expertise

- structuring and scripting the whole thing, including timings, panellists' introductions and questions to help drive the chat
- attending a meeting or conference call with panellists
- dealing with the audiovisual team on the day/handling microphones
- setting up the theme before the discussion starts, so the audience knows what they're going to get and wants to listen
- introducing the panellists
- asking the questions and keeping it going
- encouraging rapport and energy from the panellists
- making sure everyone has a fair share of the time
- keeping the discussion going
- keeping it running on time
- facilitating the Q&A section
- dealing with the unexpected
- wrapping up the discussion with thank-yous and closing off the event or handing back to someone else.

That's quite a list, isn't it? Many of those things may lie outside of your day-to-day experience too, which makes it all the more difficult to know exactly how to approach the job.

It's like you could do with a section of a book or something that would tell you more... hang on...

So, let's make it less daunting with some ideas on how to tame the beast that is panel chairing.

Before the event

Once you're marked down as the chair of the panel discussion, the event organiser should communicate with you the ideas behind or context for the discussion, the general theme or title of the panel and the date, time and duration of it.

You should also get a steer on what sorts of things they would like covered during the panel discussion. You may or may not agree, so you are perfectly entitled to offer your own suggestions as to what you think the audience would be interested in and run it by them.

The organiser will also tell you who they've booked to be on the panel and why, i.e. what that person adds. Sometimes there are people who quite clearly will only be able to comment on a certain aspect or specialist area of the discussion, so ensure you've got a couple of questions for them.

Top tip: As soon as you agree to chair a panel it becomes your show – so start owning it. You have enormous influence right now, and it's your job to think through what the audience wants to know about.

Diversity

If you feel there needs to be more gender or racial diversity on the panel, and feel you can say so, then say so. The last thing you want to be caught up in is negative publicity surrounding the line-up. For example, all-male panels (manels) or all white panels are huge no-nos and ultimately do not reflect the audience they aim to serve.

Top tip: You could offer your own suggestions of names – whenever I do this, it's always taken very positively and organisers are grateful for the help.

Microphones

Find out about the microphone situation. You may have no control over it, but forewarned is forearmed – and the panellists may well ask you about this. The ideal situation is lapel mics for everyone, table-mounted mics or handheld mics for everyone.

The worst case is that your panellists have to share a handheld mic, which turns into a 'talking stick' as a result and can stymie the flow of conversation.

Top tip: If the microphones are causing any issues, ask the audience if they can hear OK.

Dealing with the panellists

Once the panel line-up is confirmed, make contact with the panellists. Depending on the organiser, there might be a conference call or short meeting booked in for you to meet each other and share the topics for discussion.

And once the overarching theme is confirmed, you can begin to think about:

► How to 'chunk' the theme into smaller topic areas of questioning.

► What your actual questions will be, and how you might follow up, as well as specific questions for each panellist that will enable them to share a bit of their specialism, or demonstrate their point of difference.

► Anything 'newsy' or topical you need to mention that fits with what you'll be talking about (new legislation, latest invention – just do a Google News search for articles that are relevant).

► How you can include everyone from the get-go. The

opposite of this is allowing one person at the start to dominate the airtime available by going on and on. Or worse, by asking one person a few questions, before you get to anyone else. It makes everyone in the room uncomfortable, and the other panellists are sitting there like lemons, waiting for their turn.

It's up to you whether or not you share your specific questions in advance. If you choose to do this, you should warn them that you might not get around to asking all of those questions, and the topics might divert into other areas.

The risk of sharing your exact questions (rather than areas of questioning) is that panellists prepare for them in detail, and then may be disappointed or wrong-footed if those particular questions don't get asked.

Keep up communication with them – not loads, just once to say hello and that you'll be in touch soon, and then before the event, either a week or a couple of days, to check in and update them on your script/order of events/microphones.

Make sure they've got information like what time they are expected to turn up and the emergency contact number for the organiser. There will always be one person who skids in last minute, or doesn't show up at all. C'est la vie.

Top tip: Ask your panellists to think of plenty of really good examples from 'a time when' that will help the audience and frankly make for a much more interesting discussion!

Structuring and scripting

A well-structured panel discussion can really lift an event. Good signposting of the topics makes the audience feel confident that you know what you're doing and that you're in control. I find a script really helpful to keep on top of what's going on and can keep everything running to time.

It helps me map out the discussion, helps me know where I'm at. These are my script and structure suggestions:

▶ On your script – at the beginning *and* the end – write the names of the panellists, the title of the discussion, etc... so when nerves and adrenaline get the better of you, you don't need to struggle to remember who's who.

▶ Put actual times down, so if you're due to start at 6 pm, put 6 pm, then 6.10 pm next topic, 6.20 pm next topic, 6.30–6.45 pm Q&A, 7 pm ends.

▶ Break it down into subject areas, come up with five or six questions on each, and expect to get through two or three (but if your panellists are shy, or not particularly expansive, you'll end up getting through more).

▶ Consider duration for each subject area and move it on once the time is up, otherwise you'll end up running out of time to cover everything. It might also seem weighted towards one thing.

▶ Signpost the next topic with phrases like:
  ▷ 'Right, let's move on to our next subject for discussion...'
  ▷ 'I'm glad you mentioned that, because I want to know more about...'
  ▷ 'We'll have to hold that thought because we should really move on to...'

As the panel chair, it's perfectly acceptable to have your script with you, and a pen for making notes. Print it out in

14-point font, with 1.5 line spacing, if that makes it easier to read.

You might want to use a clipboard or staple it to keep your script together, so you don't inadvertently reorder the pages.

Top tip: Put your name and mobile number at the top of the script, in case you leave it somewhere in the room and end up in a panic.

Resource: You can find one of my panel chair scripts on the website makeyourselfalittlebitfamous.com as an example of how I lay out all the information I need on the day.

At the event

It's now really over to you to foster a supportive and upbeat atmosphere for the panellists and the audience. Greet them, check they're all OK and have everything they need. Like a party host.

If you get an opportunity, check the stage and seats are laid out how you'd like them. Change them yourself if not or ask the organiser to do so during the break, if the audience is still in the room.

Think about how the panellists will interact with each other when they're seated. For example, if the chairs are in a row, they will struggle to look at each other, and the person in the middle will have to do a lot of neck swivels. An arc shape for your chairs is best.

As for where you'll sit, my preference is to be to one side of the panellists, on a chair. Sometimes, there isn't a chair for you – so you'll be stood up at a lectern, or to one side. No big deal if that's the case, but don't loom over the panellists.

Once you're all up on stage, settling into your tub chairs

(nine times out of ten, they are tub chairs), it'll be time to really step up into 'ringmaster' mode. Here's how you can get it to work for you.

Introducing yourself and the theme

Sometimes there will be someone to do the job of introducing you as the panel chair, or you might be on your own. As a panel chair you don't get much opportunity to let people know what you do, so this intro is important for you.

If you're being introduced, write an intro and hand it to whoever's introducing you. If you're straight onto the stage, then it's polite to say who you are, and that you're excited/interested to be part of the event, etc. Either way, prepare something.

Then, remind the audience what the theme of the panel discussion is – set out the stall for the next hour or so of their lives... How will you introduce it so your audience really wants to listen?

You could do one or all of these:

► Bring in your own experiences as to why you feel it's important/interesting.
► Mention the latest news on the topic/up-to-date stats/industry findings.
► Talk about the topic from the audience perspective: why is it important to them? Give a sense of urgency and importance.
► Put it into context by mentioning political/social news events from the year/month/week.

At this point, you're quite obviously in charge, and nervous panellists will look to you for support and guidance. Give yourself permission to be a leader and run the show as you see fit; the others will raise their game too.

Introducing the panellists

For ideas about structuring pithy introductions that get right to the point, check out page 93.

However, in terms of plotting the way you introduce them here are a few suggestions. You might come up with your own, but these are my tried and tested methods:

Option 1: Introduce them as above and then ask them each a question, having prepped them to give a pithy (even fun!) 30–60 second answer.

The question you ask them can be light hearted, referring to something in their biog about cycling to Land's End, etc... The advantage of doing it this way is the panellist gets to warm up a bit and the audience becomes familiar with their voice.

Option 2: Introduce them each in turn until you've done everyone, and then start asking your questions. The advantage of doing it this way is that you're in complete control, and no one is going to go off on a tangent if you ask them something, having forgotten the instruction to keep it brief. This option is good if you're tight on time.

I suggest doing this with lots of energy and pace, otherwise it's a lot of sitting through each other's introductions and it can feel a bit awkward.

Option 3: Get them to introduce themselves, but manage this rather than leave it to chance by priming them to be snappy and to the point. So: who are they, where they work, how they help people and what they are passionate about. Done.

Top tip: Practise reading your intros out loud, projecting your voice and enunciating it well, so you are familiar with the script.

Handling audience questions

So, you're getting towards the end of an energised and interesting discussion. The panellists have had their say and now it's time to throw it over to the audience.

There are a number of scenarios to expect and handle:

Scenario 1: You say, 'Let's get some questions from our audience...' but you are met with silence.

This doesn't have to be the case because any event organiser worth their salt will have thought to plant a few questions for their team or a known audience member to ask. Just find out about this beforehand.

If you need to, you can revert to your own questions and get around the awkwardness with an upbeat:

'While you have a think, there's one thing I've always wanted to know about and that's...'

And then you can fill a bit while the audience sorts itself out and try again in a moment. If there really are no questions, just bring it to an early close.

Scenario 2: A woolly question you don't quite understand that's actually a comment.

This is when an audience member stands up with the roving microphone and it turns out their 'question' is more of a comment. This often happens, can be quite complex and usually goes on a bit too. But just ask a panel member to respond. Someone will have something to say.

Scenario 3: Lots of questions – yay!

This is great, but keep an eye on time and manage expectations by asking for brief questions if necessary, and especially towards the end (and brief answers). You could also assertively manage the time by saying 'we've just got time for two more questions'.

If you get anything offensive, rude or challenging then you need to deal with it firmly and move it on.

'Well thank you for that, but I think that's for another time… let's take another question.'

Top tip: If the question is simply a *bit* controversial, then bring it on! Audiences relish a bit of a heated debate and it certainly helps to reinvigorate the room.

Wrapping it all up

Never underestimate the importance of finishing on time – the audience will thank you for it – and make it your mission to do so. Even with 30 seconds to go, you can indicate to whoever is speaking to bring it to a close and then wrap up.

Even if you make it to the finish line bang on time, there's a danger that you'll have been concentrating so hard on finishing on time and remembering everyone's name to thank them that the end of your panel discussion is a bit of a washout.

Like at the end of any 'show' you want to finish on a high. Avoid 'well that's it, we're out of time, thanks very much' and letting everyone drift off.

In my view, it's far better to take control of the end of your show in the same way you took control at the start. And it should have as much energy as at the beginning.

You're the captain of the ship and it's time to dock the thing and take the glory. So, close the show down, with aplomb!

- ► Refer to any housekeeping points, like feedback or social media, or the next event – anything the organiser wants you to point out.
- ► Say what's immediately happening next (usually drinks and networking) if that's relevant to the setting.
- ► Finally, say who you've been, and thank all the panellists. The point of doing this last is that you finish with applause and everyone can get up and get on with the rest of their lives on a high.

JESSIE MADE HERSELF A LITTLE BIT FAMOUS... AS A PANEL CHAIR

The *Times* journalist and author Jessie Hewitson had been asked to chair a panel discussing autism with an audience of 200 people. Her son is autistic and Jessie had just published her book *Autism: How to Raise a Happy Autistic Child*, which features adults with autism, and their experiences and insight.

She knew it would be a chance to get exposure for her book and reach more parents of people with autism.

As Jessie hadn't done any public speaking before, she was nervous and asked me to give her some pointers on chairing a panel discussion, so she could make the very most of the opportunity. My training gave her permission to run the show the way she wanted to, and to 'own it'. She emailed me the next day and said:

"I did what you said, I scripted the whole thing and kept it running to time as a result. I had my say, and directed the conversation. At the end, the organiser said she couldn't believe it was my first time chairing a panel. I'm certainly going to do more of this as I really enjoyed it."

As well as enjoying it on the day, which is a real bonus, Jessie now speaks in public on a regular basis. Which is, according to her:

"Amazing, considering I used to find even speaking in some meetings intimidating. I've now got the confidence and skills I needed to tackle this fear."

Five top tips for being a brilliant panel chair

- ▶ Smile, breathe, bring energy to the room – enjoy your moment.
- ▶ Be fully engaged in the subject under discussion.
- ▶ Be bang up to date.
- ▶ Keep on top of your timings, don't let them gab on.
- ▶ Be mindful that your panellists may be nervous – be encouraging.

If you remember nothing else, remember this

You are the greatest showman. Well, you're not, that was Hugh Jackman, but you are kind of like the ringmaster – it's your show, own it!

How to get on a panel in the first place

Unless you want to practise in front of the mirror at home for evermore, you'll need to actually get on some panels to try out what you've learned. In an ideal world, you'd be invited to take part in a panel. You'd blush, say 'aw shucks, I'll check my diary' and then say a very loud 'yes'.

But people don't always ask out of the blue because they might not know you, or don't think you'd be interested. Or, they consider you to be too high up and too busy to be bothered with them. So, you've got to put it out there that you're a person who's willing and keen to be involved. It's up to you to be proactive and ask the people who are organising events and putting on panels.

Be panel aware

A basic starting point is to become 'panel aware'. When are they happening and who's putting them on? Keep your eyes peeled and your ears open. Attend things, sign up for lists that might tell you about 'stuff that's happening'. Pay attention and be on red alert for the words 'panel' and 'discussion' so you get to know the landscape and where the opportunities might be.

For example, if you've attended a conference in the past, you'll probably be notified of the next one. You'll get an email from the organisers, telling you the date, location and the speaker line-up. They'll also say it's going to be amazing, and tell you how you can buy a ticket.

Create an events folder

Managing the marketing emails about events is usually done by pressing delete, isn't it? But actually, they can be very useful to you in furthering your career as a panel contributor or panel chair.

It's a two-minute job to create an 'events I could appear at' folder – either on email or on a computer drive. Or in something purpose built like the Evernote app. Swish it across and look at it later when you're motivated to 'get out there'.

Get in touch

When you have information, you can then make contact with the organiser. If there's not an opportunity for you on this occasion, then could they bear you in mind for the future?

If it's relevant to you, and you feel you can offer something that adds value, then contact the organiser and say that you'd be happy to take part in any panel discussion taking place as part of the conference. Send them a short biog and tell them why you're passionate about the subject/industry issue.

Big or small, it doesn't matter

It doesn't have to be a big conference (they can be quite hard to get into, unless you're a paying sponsor or are connected somehow with the event or organiser) – it could be a local event, an event your company or organisation is putting on, or an association or networking group that meets regularly.

In fact, if you're starting out, you probably don't want to be offering yourself up to 'the industry's biggest annual event, globally' do you? Start small, local, and use it as a sandpit.

Stalk them on social media

As well as calling or emailing them directly to offer your services, connect with them by jumping on LinkedIn to say hi, follow them on Twitter, like their Instagram stuff. Be a super-friendly, keen bean!

They will remember you and want you to take part because they'll see you as plucky and enthusiastic – there is nothing more attractive than that to an event organiser!

Tell your people

If you're part of a large organisation you'll more than likely have a marketing department or press and publicity team (or both) who you can approach to let them know you're up for taking part in panels. Why tell them? Well, they are likely to field calls from event organisers requesting people to speak or take part.

You might feel that you're too junior, or lack experience of panel discussions; well I say to hell with that. You could be just the person they're looking for and unless they know you're keen, they won't know to suggest you.

Likewise, if you run a business, start telling your friends and contacts that you want to get involved with panel discussions and have they got any suggestions or ideas – and can they keep their eyes peeled and their ears open on your behalf?

chapter 6

MAKE YOURSELF A LITTLE BIT FAMOUS... ON TV AND RADIO

Does anyone have any questions for my answers?

Henry Kissinger

Being interviewed on TV or radio is good for building profile. It's good for your organisation's brand, and it's good for you as an individual. Because the minute you are seen on air, you are deemed more expert than you were before. I know, it's ridiculous, isn't it?

But for whatever reason, the exclusive nature of being 'a person who is deemed worthy of a broadcast media appearance' gives you instant credibility. It acts as an endorsement of your knowledge, experience and passion. And to be perfectly frank, it's still seen as a well glam thing to do.

Despite the rise in popularity of streaming services such as Netflix and Amazon Prime, traditional terrestrial broadcasters' morning and nightly news shows still reach millions of viewers and listeners every week. Appearing on television or radio carries a lot of weight – it is still impressive.

You only have to appear once, for just a few minutes, and colleagues and contacts will be queueing up to pat you on the back and say, 'Well done, you were great!'

When you get on air, and get seen, one rather amusing thing to watch out for is when you bump into an industry competitor after an appearance. They tend to say just this: 'I saw you on TV/heard you on the radio this morning.'

And then they say nothing. But if you watch very closely, they will press their lips into what I call 'cat's bum-hole mouth', revealing a whole heap of envy.

So, the benefits of appearing on TV and radio are easy enough to see: you easily increase your status as someone who knows what they're talking about; you raise your brand profile; and you piss off your competitors – what's not to like!

However, I see people having to deal with a huge stumbling block. And that stumbling block, I'm afraid to say, is you. The thing is, you more than likely hold some beliefs about the whole thing, and how you might fit into 'the media'.

You don't believe that you could 'be the one' to appear. You don't believe you could do a good job of it. You question your levels of expertise, when there are others who know more about your topic.

Hopefully, what I am going to share with you over the course of the next few pages will give you the confidence to think differently about all of that.

Who is it for?

So, this chapter is for all levels of experience:

▶ If you have already been on TV and radio, and want to make a better fist of it next time.
▶ If you find yourself spending an unnecessary amount of time preparing for the interviews.
▶ If you haven't been on air yet, and you fancy having a go. This is an overview of how it all works and how you can get on.
▶ Or, you're thinking 'No way, Penny, you must be off your head, the bright lights and cameras of the media aren't for me!'. I say, keep an open mind, because you never know when the Lady Fame might come a callin'. Plus, the

tips and techniques in this section are applicable whenever you're communicating via a medium that isn't in person, face to face. For example, on a conference call, webinar presentation or company website video.

Whatever your experience, I hope you're itching to read this section anyway, because, let's face it, being on TV and radio is the sexiest bit of the book! It's traditionally one of the most glamorous and aspirational ways to make yourself a little bit famous. Apart from owning the biggest yacht in Monaco and flouncing around on deck all day in a feather boa.

It's also shrouded in mystery – like skiing or parenthood or owning a dog – until you actually do it, you can't quite imagine it.

Nerves and adrenaline – now you're talking!

So, you *might* have seen me, when I was on TV, presenting the business bulletin bit on BBC *Breakfast* or the News Channel. If so, you probably thought 'What a pro – such a slick performer, where did Penny learn to be so great?' Am I right, yes?

Well, I'll have you know that I was quite the opposite of that smug and glamorous television presenter stereotype. I have walked a mile in the shoes of someone who is nervous, anxious, hyper adrenalised, unsupported and poorly guided. Knocking knees and eye twitches were everyday occurrences. In broadcast journalism at the BBC, when I was there anyway, it was sink or swim. You can or you can't. There didn't seem to be room for anything in between, or for airing your fears and insecurities.

The bulk of my problem came from having had zero

training before I found myself on camera, fronting a couple of *Panorama* programmes on BBC1. (That'll be the flagship investigative documentary programme *Panorama*. I know, right, like, OMG!)

The training input had also been zero when I later found myself presenting live, on national breakfast television.

Although I had had plenty of experience on live radio, the difference between the two mediums is enormous. On radio, you don't have to worry if your flies are down or if you've got spinach in your teeth, and many of the older gentlemen presenters really don't.

You don't have to smile, give eye contact and speak into a camera lens; you can make notes as you go when you're interviewing someone; and you can mime hand signals to your producer (like shrugging your shoulders, pulling a face, pointing at your watch, or doing the 'let's go for a drink after the show' hand gesture).

I'm not going to lie, when I first started presenting on live TV I felt like I was driving a car. Having never driven before. At 100 miles per hour, along a busy motorway. Trust me, that is not a nice feeling. I simply observed as much as I could, and watched and learned from colleagues. What else could I do?

So, more than most media professionals, I reckon, I truly understand that the prospect of appearing on a television or radio programme can keep you awake at night. Nerves and adrenaline at full tilt – and it's a very natural reaction to what is a very unnatural situation.

When I run my media training sessions, I begin by asking the delegates in the room what concerns them most about being interviewed on TV and radio. What might cause them anxiety dreams the night before taking part in a live broadcast. We get it all out there and write a list on a flip chart. This is what people worry about:

- ► saying the wrong thing
- ► looking stupid/like an idiot
- ► not knowing the questions in advance
- ► not knowing what to say
- ► not understanding the question
- ► going on for too long
- ► getting tongue tied, or completely blanking
- ► not getting all their point across
- ► what to wear.

Feel familiar? Even if you have no desire to be on air, these things are easy to imagine. And that list stems from the most basic of reactions to a situation we don't have full control over. There's the fear of failure (cocking it up, live on air) and the fear of rejection (not being good enough). It's the classic stuff that makes us human.

At the end of the media training day I check in with the delegates, to see just how many of the concerns on the list have been expunged. And more often than not, it's all of them.

Funny how a bit of knowledge, some actual interview practice in front of a camera and their fears have vanished! In fact, things are completely different – my course attendees tend to finish the day keen as mustard to get on air. Excited to appear on television or radio to share their knowledge, experience and passion – because they know how to do it really well!

And importantly, they feel in control. Well, more in control than when they arrived that morning. And that's what I hope you'll feel when you read this section of the book. The last thing I want is for you to feel like I did when I first started on the airwaves – vulnerable, nervous, adrenalised and at the wheel of a car that's going too fast.

The airwaves and news programmes

My realm of experience comes from years in TV and radio, so I will mostly refer to the *broadcast* media. Although you can also apply what you learn in this chapter to print media interviews.

I will also refer to *news* programmes, because that's where interviewees are in hot demand, around the clock. They are a staple of a broadcaster's schedule. The breakfast shows, the 'drivetime' programmes, the daily magazine shows and rolling news channels – all tackle the day's news and current affairs topics, and, crucially, they hoover up guests like you wouldn't believe.

That's not to discount opportunities to appear on other types of shows, such as phone-ins, lifestyle or feature programmes, local community or Internet-only radio stations. The following practical advice lends itself to any situation where you are being asked questions and need to come up with something interesting to say.

On-air experts

There are hours and hours of airtime, so the broadcasters' aim is to get bums on seats to fill that time. I'm here to tell you how you can be that bum.

For the purposes of this chapter I'm going to work on the

idea that you want to be a regularly called upon go-to expert. In my experience, it is the most fruitful space a freelancer, author, speaker, business owner or senior leader can occupy, in media terms.

I'm referring to the person who is invited for interview to help explain a story, give industry or sector insight and suggest a reasonable response to something. They are there to help us understand the story, and what to think about it. They bring their perspective, and that's why they're asked on.

Contrast that with the reporters, correspondents or presenters on the show. They are there to provide neutral information – they aren't allowed to air their opinions.

There are a range of other people who are interviewed, who I wouldn't define as experts. For example, 'the author of a report, or new book', 'the chief executive of the company' or 'a politician with a policy announcement'. These types of interviewee tend to appear only once in a while, by virtue of the fact they are part of the story – they aren't commenting on it.

So, who are these go-to experts? Well, they are people like you. They are concise, compelling and seemingly confident. And they are in demand, to help fill airtime.

Please note that radio stations and TV channels have their own vernacular when referring to this role: you might hear the word 'pundit', 'contributor', 'guest' or 'commentator', for example.

JUSTIN MADE HIMSELF A LITTLE BIT FAMOUS... ON TV AND RADIO

Justin Urquart Stewart is the co-founder and a director of 7iM, a company that helps people invest their money. He's been on air, as an expert, for as long as I can remember. He receives calls at all times of the night and day from programme makers wanting him to go on air and share his knowledge as a financial expert.

I met Justin when I was a junior researcher on a BBC2 daytime show called *Working Lunch*, in the mid-90s. At the time, he worked for Barclays' investment arm.

He'd be invited onto our programme to help viewers understand the latest twists and turns in the stock market, what the trends were for investing in different sectors, any surprise dips in company share prices, pensions and savings, and so on.

He was commenting on the news, he wasn't part of it – and he was tapping into a rich seam of opportunity to appear. As a result, Justin is still booked, as a go-to expert contributor, to this day and sees it as part of his job:

'As the figurehead for my business, I'm in a good position to get more profile for the brand. Being a regular commentator serves 7iM really well, as it served Barclays when I worked there.'

Justin and I have become pals over the years, which is no surprise because he's super friendly and helpful. I saw him recently at his office in London, where he showed me a line graph he'd put together. It measured all of his media activity in 2016; the TV and radio appearances, the number of newspaper articles in which he was quoted, and the many online quotes too.

The graph also showed how much his company would have forked out had they paid for the coverage. And get this, they estimated it would have cost over £250k per month for equivalent advertising. Or £3m for the year.

In reality, Justin's only expenditure was his time.

Not only would that level of profile have been costly, it would have been almost impossible to achieve. Justin is regularly interviewed for three, four or five minutes at a time – compare that with TV and radio ads that are just 30 seconds long.

He gets quality airtime, and unlike a salesy advert, he is actually useful. Sharing his knowledge, experience and passion and helping programme makers fill their airtime. For his efforts he is treated with respect and gratitude, and deemed an expert by viewers and listeners – what PR or marketing or advertising campaign nets you that?

And even if Justin's company press office wrote the best press releases and took journalists out to dinner, or to the races, he *still* wouldn't achieve that level or duration of airtime. Why? Because there are far more opportunities for an expert to appear, to comment *on* the news, than when you're *in* the news.

So, unless you have a spare few million quid to spend on advertising and PR, read on. I'm going to cover the following five areas to help you make yourself a little bit famous on TV and radio:

▶ What the media wants and how you can help
▶ Pre-interview preparation
▶ Performing on TV and radio
▶ Answering a call from a journalist
▶ Getting on TV and radio in the first place

Above all, I aim to give you confidence because at the end of the day we're just dealing with a bit of broadcasting. It's easy to lose perspective when nerves turn you stupid and it's worth being reminded that going on TV or radio isn't quite the same pressure as performing open heart surgery.

What the media wants and how you can help

The broadcast media wants good stories and really good interviewees to talk about those stories. The more relevant you are to them and the more helpful you can be, the more likely it is that you will end up one of their go-to experts.

A good interviewee

The idea of a journalist getting out into the real world, to meet and develop new contacts, is a bit of a myth – or at the very least, an irregular occurrence. They simply don't have the time or resources.

Whenever I was booking guests for the programmes I worked on, I would pretty much turn to the same old faces and voices. In fact, some of those faces and voices are still invited on air now, over 20 years later.

Media people are hugely grateful to good interviewees – even if they don't show it. It means they've filled airtime and ticked something off their huge to-do list – who doesn't like that?

So, what makes 'a good interviewee'? If you're booked onto a programme, and it's your first time, the producer will have their fingers crossed that you:

- ► fit into the style, pace, tone of the show
- ► are polished, confident and bring energy to your interview
- ► say some interesting stuff
- ► have passion and reasonable opinions
- ► explain information clearly, simplifying the complex without 'dumbing down'
- ► outline the impact of the subject in hand.

Could you tick those boxes? If you're in business yourself, or have ambition for your career or organisation, then you no doubt behave and communicate in this way every day anyway. But a good interviewee isn't simply someone who can 'do a good turn' when they are being asked questions on the programme. A good interviewee is someone who is easily found and whose expertise is easily recognisable.

The importance of being expert

Remember Jay Klein, the chewing gum guy I patronised in Monaco? His general 'campaign issues' were around sugar and artificial sweetener. By focusing on topics that have broad appeal to a wider audience – and nothing to do with what he sells or his business – building the brand profile of the PUR Company has been made easier.

Klein might be invited on TV and radio programmes in January following the season of excess – too much sugar! He may also be asked to take part in programmes to discuss a news story about diabetes, or obesity, or aspartame. He's knowledgeable, with experience, and is passionate.

So, can you stand out as an expert? Are you associating with relevant topics online, sharing ideas on your subject matter or campaign issues? Help make the 'fit', between you and a story, really obvious. Being a good interviewee means being found in the first place, and then doing a good turn when the actual camera or microphone is live.

Jay Klein is a 'good interviewee' in that he's known for having expertise in a certain subject area, *and* he's a good performer.

There we have it, that's what the media wants, when it

comes to the bums on seats – good interviewees. It's as simple as that. Have a think about what you could do to help and how you could fit in.

Five top tips for what the media wants and how you can help

▶ Make notes about the types of stories different programmes and stations cover.

▶ Listen out for the style, pace and tone of different programmes, so you can fit in nicely.

▶ Fashion yourself as an expert in something, so it's easy for programme makers to 'join the dots' of why you're the person for the job.

▶ Associate heavily with your subject area specialism, be congruent when someone looks at your LinkedIn profile, or the stuff you share on Twitter.

▶ Practice at having opinions out loud – what would you say, and how would you say it, if you were the interviewee?

If you remember nothing else, remember this

The media needs bums on seats in order to fill airtime. There is demand for bums like you.

Pre-interview preparation

There's a regular go-to expert on British TV and radio called Henry Pryor. You might have seen him on TV or heard him on radio. He's often called up, like Justin Urquart Stewart, when there's a story that needs an expert opinion. Henry's 'thing' is property – so for any property latest, he's a great choice to have on your programme. He can comment on changes to the interest rate, mortgage lending figures, government schemes to invest in building, negative equity, rental market issues, and so on.

One day, before interviewing him on *BBC Breakfast*, Henry told me about the rule of thumb he uses when getting ready for interviews:

'Prepare three interesting things to say, expect to say two of them.'

There's a bit of an art to preparing 'stuff to say' for TV or radio appearances. One trap I notice people falling into is that they spend way too much time on preparation and end up over-prepared and rather wooden in their performance.

So here are my pointers for easy and efficient preparation for media appearances.

Work out how long you'll get

Before you get your notepad and pencil out, start by working out how long you're going to have to talk.

You can do this by watching or listening to previous programmes and identifying what happens. If you've been told you're going to be interviewed at 8.25am, then listen to the last five days of the 8.25am slot. Get a sense of the duration of the interview and how many questions are asked in that time.

The table overleaf shows approximate interview durations on daily television and radio programmes.

For example, if you've been asked to do a pre-recorded interview that's going to end up in a report on one of the nightly TV news programmes, what you say will get edited down to a 15–30 second clip of you talking. Therefore don't work hard preparing yards of material. Instead, craft a few short pithy statements that are choc-full of what you want to say. Make every word count.

	Daily TV news	Daily radio news
Style	Always brief	Usually brief
Live interviews	2–4 mins	3–5 mins
Studio environment	Busy, intimidating	Relaxed, one-on-one
Pre-recs	Involved, inconvenient	Simple, quick
Pre-rec edited clips	15-30 secs	30-60 secs
Down the line	Fixed camera	ISDN/telephone

How much notice will I get?

People are always surprised at how little notice they get for an appearance on television or radio. You might get a call the day before, or just a few hours ahead of going live on air. Apologies for freaking you out if you weren't aware of that before now.

But if you think about it for a moment it's not surprising, given that daily news programmes are just that – new. They are mostly 'put together' the day before, or the morning of transmission. There's an element of planning, sure, but as the day or the hour gets closer, the detail of what and who is going in a programme is tweaked right up to the eleventh hour.

Use FACE to prepare

Remember FACE from chapter 3? It helpfully brings your facts and the details, your opinions and real-world examples, to the front of your mind – so you're not mentally reaching for them when the red bulb on the camera or microphone lights up and you're on! So, make FACE your friend for media appearances, it really does help.

It also helps when you're short on time and the pressure is on. Put FACE on the back of an envelope and you can quickly and easily prepare your thoughts, no matter how short the notice.

Do I get the questions in advance?

Oh, what a sweet question, but no, you don't get the questions in advance. You may think that unfair, or that there's some sort of conspiracy to 'catch you out' with unknown questions, but the reality is this:

▶ The questions haven't been written yet. The time-poor journalist you spoke to is on a deadline and busy setting up several story items at once.

▶ They have been written, but they may change. There is always a chance a story will 'move on' a bit or unfold before it gets to air.

▶ Or, the questions have been written and are perfectly up to date, but the presenter decides to ask you different questions, reorder them or rephrase them. The danger is if you knew them, and had prepared accordingly, that might throw you off your game.

(The first reason is the most common, in my experience.)

But bear this in mind: you help shape the questions anyway. When a researcher/producer/reporter rings you up to ask if you'll come on air, they also ask what you think or what you might say. You'll have told them your reaction and thoughts on the story, and a bit about your experience. So, the questions are based on what you've already said. You've shared your knowledge; the questions are there almost to prompt you to say it again.

If you get the chance – just before going on air – it's perfectly acceptable to ask the producer or presenter in the studio 'What are you going to ask me about first?' Then you can order your thoughts to make a really strong start in your interview.

What if I can't get to the studio – how does that work?

It's not always possible to be in the studio, from where a programme is broadcasting. This is what happens in that circumstance:

For TV interviews, you may end up being part of a 'down-the-line' interview. You would head to one of the regionally located 'fixed line cameras' and sit in front of the camera there. The programme you are dealing with will book it and arrange for one of the staff there to act as a 'meet and greet', to help you get set up and deal with the technical side of things.

You might be on holiday in Cumbria and get a call from the News Channel to do an interview. Rather than say 'no, sorry, I'm on holiday', you could offer to drive to Carlisle city centre, to BBC Cumbria, and sit in front of the camera there to share your fabulous expertise.

Up and down the country, there are cameras with stools in front of them, just waiting for your bottom.

For radio interviews, the same applies – there's a news booth studio available in most local radio stations. You put on the headphones and start talking when you hear your name and have been asked a question. You can do live or pre-recorded interviews this way.

Technology has played a big part in making non-studio attendance possible. For TV, producers are sometimes happy to accept Skype calls. And on radio, for pre-recorded interviews, it's common to record your end of a phone interview and send the MP4 to the person who's interviewed you. They then edit it together with the recording of their voice, and end up with a quality-sounding bit of audio.

The big point in all of this is that you can make yourself available, and you don't need to be in a big city in order to do that. But if you're flexible and accommodating, it will go a long way.

How will I be introduced?

It's up to you how you're introduced but my advice would be to keep it as simple as possible. Long job titles that mean very little to the outside world are to be avoided. Just your name and organisation is sufficient. Tell whoever is booking you well in advance how you want to be introduced – the spelling and pronunciation of your name, if it's one that most people get wrong.

The interviewer usually says your name and organisation, and will perhaps explain a bit about why you're the person to be interviewed, especially if you're not from a well-known company or charity. Or it's not obvious as to what it does. For example:

'Joining me now to talk about technology in agriculture is Joanne Smith, from Fronto-ponics – a company that grows herbs without using water or natural daylight.'

If the interviewer gets any of the introductory details wrong, you could correct them if it's horribly far from the truth.

But if it's a simple mispronunciation of your name, correcting them would make you look like a bit of a pedant. Be generous, sometimes interviewers are handed the information at the last minute. The key is not to let it throw you.

Should I prepare to 'wedge in' my organisation's name?

I appreciate that's what you might call a loaded question. But attempting to say your company name, or charity strapline, or website or phone number hotline in an interview is not cool. Not just my view, but the view of most broadcasters I have worked with.

Your PR firm or press officer might have drilled you in 'getting a mention' and really want you to say '... here at Fronto-ponics, we are passionate about growing herbs that are full of flavour...'.

Hearing 'Fronto-ponics' might prompt a lap of honour round the office, but for on-air experts, expressing names and web addresses or phone numbers is not advisable. It might mean the difference between getting asked back or not.

Besides, the interviewer says your name and organisation when they introduce you. And on TV, it's there for all to see on the graphic strapline at the bottom of the screen, so what more do you want?

Rest assured, a lazy Google search of your actual name will get people to your company anyway. Or vice versa. And remember, you're not there to sell or promote anything.

Five top tips for pre-interview preparation

▶ Research the show you'll be appearing on by watching or listening to it.

▶ Calculate the duration of your interview and prepare accordingly.

▶ Use FACE to prepare some facts, comments and examples.

▶ Don't be surprised by short-notice requests.

▶ Don't wedge in references to your organisation.

If you remember nothing else, remember this

Craft and practise out loud some easy-to-say, real-world examples that help make your point.

Performing on TV and radio

I love helping people boost their performance, and confidence, in broadcast media interviews. For me, the best bit of my media training day is seeing dramatic improvements from the first round of on-camera interview practice to the second attempt.

When I was interviewing people on television and radio, I was always keen for them to do well. Smiling and nodding, encouraging them to say more about their subject, I wanted them to expand their ideas and bring in colourful examples from their world. I'd think of questions that would elicit good answers, rather than trying to trip anyone up.

'Well done, that was a great interview' I would say after hearing from someone for the first time 'You made some super points!'

So, here's a whistle-stop tour of all the tips and techniques I use to help people perform brilliantly on air so they feel like an accomplished interviewee. Once you know them, you can dispense with the uncertainties that hold you back from thinking you'd be any good at this stuff.

Where do I look when I'm on TV?

This easy-to-remember rule will stand you in good stead for whatever on-camera situation you find yourself in.

And it is this: do *not* look into the camera, unless you are told to.

If you're being interviewed in person by someone, look them in the eyes. If you dart your eyes to the camera at any point, you'll look ridiculous or plain shifty. Don't do that. It's a conversation between you and the other person; the camera in this circumstance is a voyeur.

If you are told to look down the barrel of the lens, it might be for stylistic reasons as part of the 'look' of the programme, for example in a documentary.

Or if you're doing a 'down-the-line' interview, with the interviewer in another location. You are being beamed into the studio and appear on a big screen behind or to the side of the presenter. So, don't pick your nose or swear.

To recap: do *not* look into the camera, unless you are told to. Easy peasy.

Should I smile?

It's a broadcast, not a funeral, so a bit of smiling doesn't go amiss. Smiles are attractive and make people want to listen to what you've got to say.

I know you take your subject area very seriously, of course, but you don't have to drag the depth of that seriousness around with you in order to make your point.

But I don't mean grin like a fool either. A smile and a nod when you're introduced is lovely. If you make a bit of a joke, or a lighter point, then your face should match what you're saying. You don't need to attend the Actors Studio in New York for this one, but mono-facial expressions do not entice people to want to know more.

And a smile can be heard, just like in a phone call, so it applies on the radio or on a podcast too.

If you are smiling, your vocal tone changes and becomes more positive and friendly. This attitude is infectious and will help you carry your message with more impact. Smile and your whole TV and radio audience smiles with you!

Can I take notes into the studio?

I've watched people enter the radio studio, clutching on to their notes. They put them down next to them, and before you know it they're reading them. They can't resist the temptation to refer to them. They can't help themselves.

And you know what that sounds like, don't you? Yes, it sounds like reading! Wooden and stilted, with your brain working fast to scan the page for the next thing to say. I've heard people stumble over their own handwriting.

Being interviewed on TV or radio should at least feel like a conversation – although we know it's not quite that natural. So, ask yourself, do you bring notes to a short conversation with someone? I'd hope not.

Get into the habit of remembering your stuff. You know it anyway, you've used FACE to bring the information you want to share to the front of your mind.

So no, don't take your notes into the studio.

What if I don't know the answer?

In the 1970s, the US Secretary of State, Henry Kissinger, opened a White House press conference with: 'Does anyone have any questions for my answers?'

He was boldly expressing the kind of thing you can be taught in classic media training. It's the idea you can 'pivot' away from a question you don't want to, or can't, answer and on to something you do want to talk about.

It's a nifty 'get out of jail' trick for spokespeople, perhaps on air because of a problem they've caused. Or for politicians being hauled over the coals for something they've done wrong. It's fairly obvious when they wilfully and completely avoid a question, isn't it? They'll say something like 'Look, my policy is a way for people to...' or even just ignore the question completely.

For go-to experts, like you (yes, you!), who are called upon to talk *about* the news, pivoting immediately away from a question you don't really fancy is a bit heavy handed. But equally, it's worth realising that a media interview is not an exam, so you don't have to fully answer the question.

In fact, some questions are so broad you can get stuck into any point you want to make, almost immediately. Or, from time to time, you'll hear a question that isn't very good, or it refers to a less important area (interviewers don't always know that much about the issue in hand). And occasionally, you won't know the answer.

So, for these circumstances, I recommend you use ABC: Acknowledge, Bridge and Continue. If you've had any media training, you might have come across this idea, or similar, already.

You **Acknowledge** the question: 'Well that's obviously of great interest to a lot of people...'

You **Bridge**: 'But the thing that everyone in the industry is talking about is...'

And **Continue** with your points – the stuff you've prepared using FACE, and the topics and stories you are most comfortable with.

Once you start answering the question, you're in the driving seat. You can take the conversation wherever you like. Ideally you stay in the neighbourhood of the topic – avoid driving the viewers and listeners somewhere else completely. But the turns in the road are yours to make as you see fit.

If you sound confident and make an interesting and compelling point, most people will forget the question anyway.

ABC is quite a natural progression and gives you the option of expanding on to the points you want to make. You're not pulling the wool over anyone's eyes, you're simply drawing on your prep and what you know best.

What should I wear?

When I worked in TV news, contrary to what most people think there is no wardrobe mistress or stylist helping you pick out what to wear. Nobody coordinates 'the look' of a show, not at the BBC anyway. You buy it all yourself, and you watch others to see what works.

So, how do you want to come across? Business smart, or your usual style of attire – if that is different to the mainstream?

Here's a steer to help you with your wardrobe planning ahead of a TV appearance:

► Skirts – knee length or above might look great when you're standing up, but if you're asked to sit down, the hemline will ride up and distract from what you're saying. That's fine if you want the nation looking at your legs, but I'm guessing you want to raise your profile for what you know about, not what you look like.

► Jewellery – distracting if there's too much of it, or it makes a noise. This is important for radio appearances – wearing a bangle that jangles is an unnecessary accessory!

► Ties – it's perfectly acceptable not to wear a tie these days, as long as there's a jacket, and the shirt collar is designed for non-tie wearing (no one likes the flappy loose collar look, do they?).

► Patterns – big pattern repeats are fine, small patterns and fine stripes may 'strobe' (jump around) on the screen.

► Colour – yes please, the brighter the better for TV; avoid black and dark blues if you can. If a tie is the only way of getting colour into your outfit, then ignore the point about not having to wear a tie because they really can jazz a suit up, can't they?!

► Necklines – I've seen a pussy bow-necked blouse, with a V-neck jumper on top, with a round-necked jacket on top of that. Now, that's a lot of neckline going on – which clearly distracted me from what the interviewee was saying, as I still remember it now.

► Watch and learn – most things in TV don't change much, so it's just a case of watching to see what everyone wears. And then follow suit, as it were.

Hair and make-up

Television studio lights can wash out your features and make you look a bit pale, so make-up is a must.

Before you leave for the studio, ask the researcher or journalist with whom you're dealing if there's someone who will be doing your make-up. If so, turn up nice and early in order to get 'done'.

Most local station programmes don't have the resources to provide this, so if there's no make-up artist on site, slap on a bit more than you'd usually wear. As if you're on a big night out, or going to a wedding.

If you don't wear make-up, or a lot of it, then powder is your friend. Shiny faces look sweaty, and sweaty faces look nervous. Plus, the lights will bounce off your face and distract from what you are saying.

With hair, check it's not sticking up in a weird 'bed-head' sort of a way. If you've got a lot of hair or a heavy fringe, just be careful it doesn't fall over your eyes. Unless you're that bloke from the 80s band Flock of Seagulls.

Manufacturing rapport

Rapport with your interviewer is a cool thing to have when you're on TV or radio. A connection or chemistry – albeit temporarily – is really appealing to audiences. It creates energy and helps the interviewee do their best.

But there are a couple of scenarios where you might have to create rapport yourself.

The first situation is on the radio when you find yourself talking to the top of the presenter's head. It's annoying, because you've made the effort to get to the studio, all full of nerves and adrenaline, it's your big moment and yet you barely get looked at.

It isn't because the person interviewing you is being rude on purpose, or is disinterested. They may have to get their head round what else is going on in the show, or write some questions for the next interview.

They could also be reading texts that have come in from listeners or checking the newswires on their screens.

The second situation is on TV. Rapport is normally there if you are in the studio with the interviewer, as they do have to look at you – they're also on TV. But if you're in a different studio, doing a 'down-the-line' interview, the only thing you're looking at is the camera.

So, imagine there's a smiley face on the lens of the camera and maintain eye contact with it. Smile and nod at it, as though it were a human. Your performance will better for it.

In both these circumstances pretend they are really interested in what you're saying and ignore the non-verbal body language that says otherwise. Say their name, perhaps include them in your answer, and if in doubt just keep your energy up and directed at them – regardless of the response.

Can I move my hands?

Before my first-ever live TV presenting shift on breakfast television, I'd been under the impression you shouldn't move your hands when on camera. Gesticulating was something you did in your own time, when you were off air.

There is a lot of confusion and mystery about this. As a result, it's the most frequently asked question in my media training or smartphone video courses.

So, I always share a tip the former *BBC Breakfast* presenter Bill Turnbull gave me one day. It was during the bit when the regional news comes on. It's a chance for the presenters to touch up their make-up or stretch their legs.

Bill strolled over to me at the business news table and casually asked if I used my hands when I was talking in everyday conversation.

'Yes, of course,' I said (with plenty of Italian-style hand waving).

'Then use them on camera as well,' he said. 'It'll help you be yourself, and what you say will flow much better.'

And he was right. It's old-skool media training that tells you not to use your hands – to somehow restrict them from popping up on screen. All too often the result is wooden and formal because you're concentrating on not using your hands, not what you're saying.

Bill's advice also applies if you're speaking on a stage, or appearing on or moderating a panel. *And*, bizarrely, it applies if you're on the radio – it's all about communicating as you *would do normally*. If you are a hand waver, wave them. If not, don't start.

The other reason for sharing this story is to remind you that being you, using your voice, sharing your opinions and showcasing your expertise, will help you make yourself a little bit famous.

More importantly it will give your messages passion and energy, and more likely to be heard.

So, next time you're watching TV, make a note of when people use their hands to help them make their point. It doesn't look weird, unusual or out of place, does it? In fact, it gives the impression of passion and energy.

Five top tips for performing on TV and radio

▶ Stay hydrated and don't over-caffeinate.

▶ Don't take your notes into the studio.

▶ 'Bridge' to what you know about.

▶ Smile.

▶ Be yourself; wave your arms like you just don't care.

If you remember nothing else, remember this

Don't look at the camera, unless you're told to look at the camera.

Answering a call from a journalist

This is an important moment that can make the difference between being invited on to a programme or not. Taking a call from a journalist, researcher or producer is not a case of giving yes/no answers, it is actually an audition.

When you get a call from someone who says they're working on a story for their programme, and are looking for someone to talk about it, that's your green light to expand on what you know about the topic.

You might not know the very latest news, or have not yet seen this particular twist in the story in the papers, but if it's in your subject area ballpark, you'll be fine. Express your thoughts to whoever's called you, but don't go on and on. Tell them some interesting stuff, be passionate, opinionated and give an example.

Being passionate and enthusiastic about the story is very compelling, and sometimes a relief to the time-poor, phone-bashing programme maker. If you can demonstrate this when they call, you'll have a friend for life.

When I was presenting the business bulletins on the BBC's News Channel, I found it hard to whip up enthusiasm for certain topics, especially those we had to cover on a regular basis. The UK's monthly inflation rate figures, for example. I used to think to myself: 'Oh no, not again, I care not a jot for this subject.'

But then, if I spoke to a potential on-air guest who had nothing but excitement in their voice about the prospect of inflation going up or down, I would breathe a sigh of relief. They have passion, experience and knowledge! Yay! And because of that, I wouldn't have to work too hard at pushing the inflation-story boulder up the hill for our viewers. Phew!

Someone like that would give me faith they could fill the airtime with some interesting stuff to say. And straight off the bat too, in a brief phone call.

Once you've shown enthusiasm and knowledge of your subject on the phone, it's time to get into the practical side of things. You might like to suggest some questions they could ask you, tell them how you want to be introduced, get the address of where you're going or details about establishing a 'line' between you and the programme, whether you need a taxi and who to ask for when you get there.

Swap mobile phone numbers, so you are both contactable at all times. And off you go!

Five top tips for answering a call from a journalist

- ▶ Express your thoughts about the story straight away, even if you're not asked specifically to do so.
- ▶ Be enthusiastic and friendly.
- ▶ If you are invited to interview, say yes to it, there and

then. There's no 'let me have a think about it and I'll get back to you' in this game.

▶ Or say no, if you absolutely cannot do it, but be helpful and suggest somebody else in your field.

▶ Offer some questions they could ask you.

If you remember nothing else, remember this

Getting a call from a programme maker is an unofficial audition to see if you've got something to say and might make a 'good interviewee'.

Getting on TV and radio in the first place

If you're serious about carving out a role for yourself as an expert contributor on TV and radio, there's a bit of legwork that needs to be done to get there.

I suggest these steps to becoming a regularly called upon on-air expert:

Identify your 'pet subjects'

I've talked about being a regularly called upon go-to expert in this chapter because that's where the opportunities are for appearing on TV and radio. You are more likely to be interviewed more times if you are someone who comments on the news, rather than trying to be part of it.

Let's take the example of a trouser manufacturer, why not. Rather than just sticking to the subject of trousers, they could comment on a whole host of topics of which they have experience.

They would know about employment issues, apprenticeships, the cost of importing, production costs, the ease of importing materials, exporting goods, fashion trends, productivity, changes to VAT and business rates.

The company might pay staff a higher wage than is set by the government. They might have strong views about in-work poverty and want to support the local community, from where most of their employees who make the trousers are found.

All of those topics have broad appeal, they're not about the company and what it does. Remember, 'pet subjects' need to be of interest to the wider public and lend themselves to what you want to be known for. Ask yourself:

► What is my area of expertise?
► What do I want to be known for?
► Do I have credibility in this area?

Those answers might not come that easily, so try a process of elimination in order to get a shortlist of your 'pet subjects'.

Find your 'target programmes'

If you are able to identify two or three 'target programmes' that cover stories relating to your pet subjects you increase your chance of appearing.

Which programmes interview people like you, who know your stuff? If you're an accountant, and have heard or seen another accountant on air – that's your space!

Do your research by listening to speech radio programmes – in the car, in the kitchen, giving them enough time so you become familiar with what you're hearing.

Also, watch TV news channels and programmes, mid-morning studio discussion programmes and political lunchtime shows, for example.

Discomfort zone warning: like anything new that you study it will take a bit of extra effort. It might even take you out of your comfort zone to begin with because we all become wedded to our favourite stations (no more music stations for you!) – but it will be worth it.

Pay attention to the interviews between presenters and expert contributors (*not* the politicians, celebrities, sports personalities, reporters/correspondents or company spokespeople). It will take time to build the picture, so challenge yourself, be disciplined and patient. Slowly, slowly catchy monkey.

Grab a notebook and list what you're hearing, breaking it down into component parts. Who is speaking and what are they speaking about? Is it the presenter introducing someone – if so, who? If that person then speaks, how are they describing or explaining things?

Actively listen out for:

▶ The stories or 'items' that get covered – is the programme likely to tackle your subject area?

▶ The style/tone/pace – is it upbeat or laid back, friendly or formal?

▶ The duration of the interviews, as this will influence how you prepare for your appearance on the show.

▶ How the questions are answered. Be critical; could they have done better, did the expert make sense, did the expert make you want to listen more?

▶ The content of the show – is it themed, or a mixture of different topics, how newsy/current is it, what happens when and what is the interviewer's style?

Background research

If you're a UK listener, try these programmes to work out where you might fit in.

On radio:

▶ Radio 2: *The Jeremy Vine Show* – daily from midday.

▶ Radio 4: *Today* programme – daily 6–9 am (listen out for experts, do not get distracted by controversial or combative interviews).

▶ Radio 4: Any programme (not drama or comedy): scour the website to identify relevant specialist shows for your expertise.

▶ World Service: ditto.

▶ Radio 5 Live: any time of the day or night, especially *Wake Up to Money*, *Breakfast*, *Afternoon Edition* and *Drive*.

▶ Your local radio station (especially if your customers tend to be local or you want to get some experience before doing national interviews).

▶ Use http://www.bbc.co.uk/radio/ to catch up, get the BBC iPlayer Radio app and/or use the 'Tune-in Radio' app to listen to any station, anywhere in the world.

On television:

▶ The rolling news channels, such as BBC News Channel, Sky News and Bloomberg have expert interviewees on all the time.

▶ BBC *Breakfast* always has interesting and varied guests/ topics. (Not always available on iPlayer, so record it or watch it live if necessary.)

▶ Main news shows (BBC, ITV, Channels 4 and 5) are good

for identifying different broadcast scenarios and what's required of experts (live from a location, live in the studio, or pre-recorded reporter pieces).

If you're outside the UK, the BBC's World Service is an excellent destination to hear people being interviewed, as it's almost all speech based.

You'll also have your own knowledge of what's on the radio and TV in your region or country, so apply the same approach. Listen and watch as much as you can in order to get under the skin of the broadcast landscape. And make sure the individual programmes you come across actually cover your subject area specialism.

Get in touch

Once you've worked out your pet subjects and target programmes, you are in a great position to feed the people who make them. It doesn't matter how you get in touch, it's whatever works. Here are some suggestions:

By email

You can be proactive when trying to get on TV and radio. A direct email to the programme producer or researcher is a super way to introduce yourself to people. But don't make the mistake of thinking it's enough to simply get in touch and say:

'Hi, I'm a trouser manufacturer [or whatever you do], I make trousers in my factory, they are good trousers.'

Because that's of no use whatsoever to a time-poor programme maker. It won't help them in the here and now. And that's what they need most help with: finding bums, filling programmes.

Bridge the gap by telling them that you would have been an ideal commentator on some of the stories they've featured recently. Our trouser manufacturer can help out by offering a bit more:

'Last week you covered the number of people who are working but who are locked into poverty. Next time you tackle this issue, please bear me in mind as I have something to say and can offer some insight. We pay our employees well above the national wage and we believe more employers should do the same.'

Or you can be reactive: if you spot a news story early in the day, send an email to your target programme as soon as you can. Say that you'd be happy to be interviewed, should they be covering the topic. Share a couple of lines about your credibility and give them your mobile number.

And then make sure you answer it and actually are available. There's nothing more annoying for a journalist or programme maker when the person offering themselves for comment isn't around on the day. Equally, don't be on holiday or out for the day.

By social media

Another way of getting in front of programme makers is to use social media.

On LinkedIn, you can make connections with correspondents and reporters, but this is only worth doing if they seem active on this platform. Do the same on Twitter, tagging people and programmes in, and using hashtags relevant to your subject area.

So, you could be that 'good interviewee' type, who is useful and on the ball with their topic – and share a news article with the producer/presenter/programme that may be of interest to them. Or share a relevant blog you've written that demonstrates your angle and knowledge on the issue.

Rowan Bridge is not a place, but a talented, hard-working reporter on the national radio station, BBC Radio 5 Live. Twitter is a major part of the way he finds stories and people. He uses social media a lot and has this advice for you:

'When I'm looking for an interviewee, I check Twitter to see who's talking about the story, or I'll Google it, which can also throw up relevant tweets. I'm looking for someone who's made an interesting point or who has shared a LinkedIn post or blog post that they have written which goes into a bit more detail.

'The other thing I look at is their Twitter profile, to see if they have enough credibility to be talking on the topic and are worth getting in touch with.

'New contributors and voices are welcome, because we don't just want to use the same old voices over and over again. In particular there is a push at the BBC across the organisation to use more female contributors and those from black, Asian and minority ethnic (BAME) backgrounds, to better represent and reflect our listeners.'

Direct communication on social media is a great way to make a connection – don't hide behind a press office and hope they'll have the same impact, or if you work for yourself, don't be your brand, be yourself.

And beware: you might go to the effort of tracking down your target, write a beautiful tweet or email, and then not get a response. How rude! But that doesn't mean you have been rejected. Here's why you might not hear back:

▶ The recipient isn't in need of you right now, because they're not covering the story.

- They had someone else lined up already.
- They're off sick/on leave that day.
- They've moved on to another programme.
- They can't respond to every email they get.

But don't lose heart: taking action, by sending an email or getting in touch via social media, means you are more likely to be on their radar for the next time your topic comes up. It's worth also double-checking you're emailing or tweeting the right person.

By phone
Getting hold of the right people to send stuff to isn't hard; just call up the switchboard and ask to speak to the programme team.

Do *not* call the hour before they go on air, or during their programme – they will not appreciate your call and won't have time for you. Your cunning plan will backfire.

Five top tips for getting on air

- Create your list of pet subjects.
- Keep up to date with related issues.
- Seek out programmes that cover your topics.
- Do your homework by listening and watching.
- Think about what you would say, if you were invited on.

If you remember one thing, remember this

If you don't get a reply to your email or tweet, it doesn't mean you've been rejected – keep going.

chapter 7

27 WAYS TO MAKE YOUR FAME GO A LITTLE BIT FURTHER

By now you will have got to grips with the importance of 'getting out there' and establishing yourself as someone who is knowledgeable, experienced and passionate about their topic. And you have plenty of practical techniques to deploy every time you are in front of people, making yourself a little bit famous.

But there's no escaping the fact that all of that activity can take focus, time and effort – especially if you are just starting out.

Because I am a fan of the WHO concept (the acronym, Work Hard Once, not the English rock band formed in 1964), I have a raft of tips and suggestions to help you make your fame go a little bit further.

I use or have used pretty much every single one of these for building my brand profile. Some of the ideas might not work for you, or be appropriate. But the main principle is this: if you participate in something, why leave it there? I suggest you act as your own publicist and always be asking yourself, 'How can I maximise this opportunity – what else can I squeeze from it?'

Let's say you've been asked to deliver a 20-minute talk at an industry event, tickets are going on sale soon and it's open to the public. Great news, you're going to be a little bit famous! There are two routes available to you now:

▸ You could prepare for the talk, deliver it, go home and forget all about it. Your fame flame would have burned brightly, but for all of just 20 minutes.
▸ Or, you could apply the WHO approach, use some of the following ideas and make your fame go further and your life a little easier.

Around the time of your talk:

1. Prepare for your talk, panel or media appearance but, while doing so, reflect your efforts with a post on LinkedIn, with accompanying photo.

'Up to my eyes in Post-it notes, but looking forward to sharing my thoughts on *ideas the audience needs to hear* at the Such & Such event, in June.'

2. In the pre-event communication with an organiser, you'll have been asked to provide a biog and photograph. As soon as they start marketing the event, jump on it. Make a comment when you see it on LinkedIn or retweet it on Twitter.

3. Include the link to the event in your email newsletter (if you send one out), or ask for it to be mentioned in your organisation's newsletter, before the event. Even those who won't be there on the day will be given the impression that you are the cat's whiskers and expert at what you do.

4. Email your colleagues, clients and contacts with a personal invitation to an event where you're talking. The likelihood of them being able to attend is slim, but the point isn't to get their bums on seats, it's to spread the word that you've been asked to speak.

5. Video can play a big part in helping further your fame, and using your smartphone is a smart way to make short and engaging content. So, whip out your phone in the couple of weeks *before* the event and press record:

'I'm excited to speak at the *Such & Such* event in June, where I'll be sharing my thoughts on *something super that speaks to you*...'

Share it on social media. Use the conference hashtags, and tag the organisers.

6. On the day, do another video at the event location before you speak. You could add a bit more information about what you're speaking about, that's useful – rather than it just being a look-where-I-am-today 'postcard'!

7. And/or after you've spoken, if you've got the energy for it (I know I don't, I'm quite wiped out after delivering a keynote), ask a couple of audience members if they don't mind saying a few words about your talk on video. What did they think of it, is it useful? Tell them you'll be sharing it on social media.

8. Share others' content from the event. If you're looking at social media after the event and come across photos of you on stage, then share it, retweet it, screen grab it, post it! Thank the originator and engage with them.

9. Writing a blog is another way of maximising your talk's potential, in terms of creating content. There is so much you could expand upon.

▶ Reflect a question from an audience member that would be of interest to your followers.

▶ Write about having a chat with someone who talked about the challenges they face, and which you could help with.

▶ Blog about the theme of the event: can you use that as a talking point?

10. Ask for feedback from the organiser. You've worked hard on your talk, so you want people to know that it went well.

11. On LinkedIn, connect with any audience members you met on the day or other speakers, or the producer of a TV or radio programme.

12. Boldly ask for a recommendation from people who seemed to really like your talk or contribution to the discussion.

13. If you know the person you're asking is busy, say you've taken the liberty of writing a recommendation or testimonial, that they can use or rewrite if they don't have time to pen one for you. Personally, I'm delighted when someone does this.

14. Contact the event organiser a couple of weeks after the event to find out if they've collated audience feedback about your talk. If it's good to excellent, share that fact. There are ways of doing that without being too much of a braggart:

'Been considered "good or excellent" by 98 per cent of the audience at *Such & Such* event last month – I'm flattered / chuffed to bits / humbled / proud to have been of use to so many people, talking about *that thing that was of use*...'

That may feel a bit show-offy, but used once in a while this is a great way to squeeze that last drop of content from your talk.

You might also like to:

15. Check how you come across on social media: ask a couple of savvy friends for their view if you're unsure – and then work hard to make sure it's congruent across all the platforms you're using. Put your expertise front and centre – what do you know about, have experience in and are passionate about? How do you help people?

16. Use the same headshot across all platforms. I'm surprised just how crap a lot of headshots are, so please, for me, avoid sunglasses, the pouty porn look, pets, kids, beaches, frowns. Event organisers, customers, journalists, bookers, colleagues want to see what they're getting. So be authentic you, plain and simple.

17. Make the most of the banner photos on social media – use an image of you delivering this talk or being on a panel, or on TV or radio. Why? Well because being on a stage or screen elevates your status to that of expert – at a glance. And it tells the world that you're open for business, as a speaker, panellist or TV and radio go-to expert. It's genius, isn't it?

18. Don't chuck stuff away. Keep hold of the preparation notes you made ahead of a talk, panel or TV and radio appearance.

I now have several A4 folders, the ones with clear plastic document pockets attached inside, in which I put the notes for every talk I have given. There are dozens of presentation planner grids, which I've dated and referenced by the event at which I spoke.

It means I can easily refresh my memory of the content I

delivered, and where possible, I can re-point it for the next audience.

19. Rather than speaking on a wide range of topics, focus your efforts on a couple of core areas which reflect your credentials as an 'expert'. That way you can reuse stories, facts, information, references for the next time you're doing something. Don't let your material go stale or become out of date, of course, but if you're always hopping about from one subject to the next you'll be WHAT (Working Hard All the Time)!

20. You can also repurpose the material from your talks, or your prep for panel or media appearances. Dusting off old notes can provide inspiration for a blog, an article on LinkedIn or a short smartphone video for social media.

21. There are rules in Europe (including GDPR) about collecting and storing information about people – adding names and email addresses to your database, without asking them, or without them doing it, is no longer welcome. So, you have to be more creative about 'building your list' of people who might be interested in hearing from you, via your email newsletter for example.

I take a glamorous jam jar with me when I head out to live events where I'm speaking. Yes, that's right, a jam jar. I tell people about my newsletter, when I'm on the stage, and say if they want to receive it they should put their business card in my jam jar. It makes life easier for them, and me.

22. And talking of business cards – always have yours on you.

23. Email is your friend. Send out a regular newsletter to your contacts (who have signed up for it or done so via the jam jar route) via an email manager system, like Mailchimp or Campaign Monitor.

If you're not sure what that might look like for you, then sign up to other people's and see what works well and what doesn't. There are some dreadful ones out there, so do your homework and make it good. Once you've got the hang of it, you can create them more efficiently every time.

In corporate life, sending colleagues your own email newsletter would be a bit weird, but I have heard of someone who sends her bosses a monthly round up of the profile-raising activity she's been involved with. Her seniors don't always reply, but they certainly know who she is.

24. Get set up on Twitter, LinkedIn, Instagram. Or if you're already set up, get involved. The more familiar you are with these platforms, the more adept you become and therefore it doesn't take you as long to share content, or find people – like journalists – who might be of use to you.

25. Schedule time in your diary, every day or every week, to make yourself a little bit famous. It's easy to disappear down the rabbit warren of social media, hunting down an event at which you could speak, or finding the name of an organiser to email. Little, often and focused is key here.

Set small, doable tasks for yourself, and make a note of what you achieved in that short space of time. It will soon build up – and carving out some time for this is especially important when you're starting out.

26. Recycling the content that you share on social media is classic WHO. You could be speaking at an event on Monday, sharing the photo on Twitter on Tuesday, turning it into a LinkedIn post on Wednesday. And on Thursday, Friday and Saturday, well, you could listen to old Craig David records.

27. Keep this book handy for when an opportunity comes your way. Do not share it with colleagues or lend it to unreliable family members. Tell them to get their own copy.

chapter 8

BACK TO YOU...

Well there you have it. Reasons *why you should* get out there more, and three major ways as to *how you could* make yourself a little bit famous. All you need in one book, to build your brand profile with practical tips and advice – and an occasional kick up the backside. It's been a pleasure sharing it with you.

Hold on to it, and refer to the handbook bits when you need a refresher ahead of a speaking opportunity, a panel appearance, or you're heading off to the TV or radio studios as an expert bum on a seat.

Please take advantage of the resources I've mentioned on the website **makeyourselfalittlebitfamous.com**. You'll find a FACE planner, for helping you prepare what to say; an example script for when you're chairing a panel; and the one-page grid for when you're speaking, to help you clearly structure your talks.

You can also sign up for my awesome fortnightly email that sends you fresh tips and ideas for building your brand profile and boosting your confidence. It's essentially a four-minute read that acts as a reminder to stop colouring in and sketch your future.

There is, however, one last thing we need to consider: your next steps towards making yourself a little bit famous. As I see it, you now have three options:

► EASY OPTION: Don't do any of the activity described in this book. Keep your skills on a tight leash, stay a best-kept secret and watch the competition sail on by. See if I care.

► POINTLESS OPTION: Do some of it on an ad hoc basis and wonder why nothing comes of it. Fulfil the prophecy that it's all a bit pointless and then give up, frustrated and confused.

▶ RESULTS OPTION: Find the time and focus. Push past fear, lack of confidence, concern about what others will think of you, stumbles and mistakes, and enjoy ultimate world domination.

I'm a fan of the latter, of course. I have seen people run with this, seek opportunities to 'get out there' and use the learning laid out in this book to great effect. It has benefited their businesses, their organisations and their careers.

So, whatever your reason is for wanting to get out there more – JFDI. The point I'm pressing is that you can't leave this stuff to chance.

Plan the work. Work the plan. And remember, you are fabulous and deserve every little bit of fame coming your way.